Leadership, Ethics and Schooling for Social Justice

Issues of social justice and equity in the field of educational leadership have become more salient in recent years. The unprecedented diversity, uncertainty and rapid social change of the contemporary global era are generating new and unfamiliar equity questions and challenges for schools and their leaders. In order to understand the moral and ethical complexity of work undertaken in the name of social justice and equity in diverse contexts, this book uses a range of different theoretical tools from the work of Michel Foucault. Rather than a prescriptive, best-practice approach to leadership and social justice, this book draws on Foucault's fourfold ethical framework, and specifically on the notions of advocacy, truth-telling and counter-conduct, to critically examine the leadership work undertaken in case studies in schools in Australia and England.

Our approach makes transparent the ethical work that leaders in these contexts conduct on themselves towards creating schools that can address the equity challenges of the present climate. It illuminates and enables critical analysis of the moral imperatives shaping the equity work of school leaders and, in particular, the possibilities for transformative leadership that can work to create schools and school systems that are more socially just.

Overall, the book's key aims are to:

- provide an innovative and comprehensive theorising of leadership for social justice in contemporary times;
- explicate the utility of key elements of Foucault's theorising of the ethical self to the domain of educational leadership; and
- provide significant practical insight into the social justice possibilities of school leadership in contemporary times through two in-depth case studies.

Richard Niesche is a senior lecturer in the School of Education at the University of New South Wales, Sydney, Australia.

Amanda Keddie is an Australian Research Council Future Fellow in the School of Education at the University of Queensland, St Lucia, Australia.

Leadership, Ethics and Schooling for Social Justice

Richard Niesche and
Amanda Keddie

Routledge
Taylor & Francis Group

LONDON AND NEW YORK

First published 2016
by Routledge
2 Park Square, Milton Park, Abingdon, Oxon OX14 4RN

and by Routledge
711 Third Avenue, New York, NY 10017

Routledge is an imprint of the Taylor & Francis Group, an informa business

British Library Cataloguing-in-Publication Data
A catalogue record for this book is available from the British Library

Library of Congress Cataloging in Publication Data
Niesche, Richard.
   Leadership, ethics and schooling for social justice / Richard Niesche and Amanda Keddie.
      pages cm
   Includes bibliographical references and index.
   1. Educational leadership—Social aspects—Australia.   2. Educational leadership—Social aspects—England.   3. Educational leadership—Moral and ethical aspects—Australia   4. Educational leadership—Moral and ethical aspects   England.   5. Social justice—Study and teaching—Australia.   6. Social justice—Study and teaching—England.
   I. Keddie, Amanda.   II. Title.
   LB2979.N54 2015
   371.20994—dc23

ISBN: 978-0-415-73662-6 (hbk)
ISBN: 978-1-315-81839-9 (ebk)

Typeset in Sabon
by Keystroke, Station Road, Codsall, Wolverhampton

MIX
Paper from
responsible sources
FSC   FSC® C013056
www.fsc.org

Printed and bound in Great Britain by
TJ International Ltd, Padstow, Cornwall

Contents

Acknowledgements

We would sincerely like to thank the participants involved in the research projects that make up this book for their time and hard work. Special thanks to Pat Thomson for her critical feedback on the manuscript, and also to Alison Lees for her help with proofreading and formatting. We would also like to thank Anna Clarkson for supporting the book as well as all the team at Routledge for their hard work in seeing this book to publication. Some parts of this book have appeared before, so we would like to acknowledge Taylor and Francis for giving permission to publish excerpts from the following: Richard Niesche (2013) 'Foucault, counter-conduct and school leadership as a form of political subjectivity', *Journal of Educational Administration and History*, 45 (2), 144–158; Amanda Keddie (2015) 'School autonomy, accountability and collaboration: a critical review', *Journal of Educational Administration and History*, 47 (1), DOI: 10.1080/00220620.2015.974146; Amanda Keddie (2014) 'School collaborations within the contemporary English education system: possibilities and constraints', *Cambridge Journal of Education*, 44 (2), 229–244; and Amanda Keddie (2012) *Educating for diversity and social justice* (Abingdon, Routledge), pages 31–33. Some of the research that appears in this book was conducted with support from the Australian Research Council Future Fellowship scheme. We officially acknowledge this support.

We would also like to thank our friends and loved ones for their patience, support and advice. In particular, Richard would like to thank Christine Mason, John and Barbara Niesche, Christina Gowlett, Scott Eacott, Jane Wilkinson and Colin Evers. Amanda would like to thank David Lees, Alexandra Keddie, Maree, Jane and Adam Cooper as well as Maria Delaney, Martin Mills and Bob Lingard. Finally, we would like to thank each other for making this collaboration an intellectually stimulating and engaging journey.

1 Introduction

So, I think I've really been able to define social justice for me as a person in the last seven months, for the first time in my career really. And maybe that's a sad indictment on the opportunities I've had in life.

(Carol)

In a sense we all have a mission statement, which is to prepare our students for the next stage in their lives, but for us that is recognising that in London, to get a job, to be a worthy and productive member of society, to have an identity, to have choices involves success in exams. It's not empty, it's very real . . . especially for us, given the state of the British economy . . . So, you know, in terms of morality, one of the things that we're most proud of from last year is that . . . every single one of [our sixteen-year-olds] is in [education], productive employment or training. And that's an achievement. And it's an Ofsted measure. And it's not a bad measure.

(Ms J)

These two quotes point to the complexities of leadership for social justice in two very different school contexts on two sides of the world. Carol is the principal of a school in a very poor urban area of Australia. Ms J is the head teacher at the Clementine Academy, the lead school of an alliance of schools in outer London. Carol refers to the processes at her school over the last seven months that have prompted her to question the privilege of her white, middle-class, Western background (like that of many principals, head teachers and teachers in Western contexts). These processes highlight for Carol how the 'opportunities' in her life arising from this privilege have sheltered her from the vastly complex and challenging circumstances of working in a very disadvantaged part of Australia. As we discuss in later chapters, this then becomes a 'call to arms' for Carol as she recognises the highly political and risky work that she needs to do to try to alleviate disadvantage, improve educational outcomes and provide the necessary support for the students in her school. This is the work of leading for social justice.

Improving educational outcomes for Ms J in her role as head of the Clementine-led alliance is a similar 'call to arms'. She views this agenda as a 'mission statement' and crucial to 'preparing students for the next stage in their lives'. Like Carol, however, as we illustrate in this book, Ms J encounters, and must navigate and overcome, many challenges and barriers in attempting to realise this social justice telos or goal.

These encounters are the key focus of this book. The comments from these two leaders highlight the need for a nuanced approach to understanding the complexity of leadership in the present moment, particularly the challenges involved in pursuing the goals of social justice. This, then, is the aim of this book: to provide a critical understanding of how leaders work in socially just ways to support schools and students to overcome disadvantage. We provide this understanding through the voices of leaders like Carol and Ms J and through the insight offered by the theoretical tools of Michel Foucault.

While critical perspectives in educational leadership have multiplied in recent years, this book makes a significant contribution to the field of educational leadership through an engagement with a variety of theoretical resources and ideas illustrated through empirical research in schools. In this book, we offer something new and different about the way leadership is being practised and undertaken in schools through a theoretically informed approach to educational leadership. While there have been a range of alternative perspectives brought into this fairly conservative and traditional field, such as gender and critical theories, and social justice, philosophical and post-structuralist approaches, few have blended an approach to researching and understanding educational leadership 'as it happens' by combining these approaches. In this book we bring together Foucault's concepts, tools and ideas not only to theorise leadership practice differently but also with particular social justice perspectives at the forefront of our thinking.

Issues of social justice and equity in the field of educational leadership have become more salient in recent years. The unprecedented diversity, uncertainty and rapid social change of the contemporary global era are generating new and unfamiliar equity questions and challenges for schools and their leaders. Framed by the current audit culture in Western education, equity for schools has become a high-stakes issue. This is perhaps most evident in the urgency around 'closing the gap' in educational outcomes between disadvantaged students and their more advantaged peers. Lingard, Sellar and Savage (2014) argue that the concept of social justice has actually been rearticulated as equity through a range of national and international testing- and data-driven accountability frameworks. Our explicit engagement with notions of social justice, power, ethics and subjectivity throughout this book signals our intention to reinsert these concepts back into the discourse of educational leadership at a time when these notions have been marginalised by highly performative governmental rationalities in many countries around the world.

Amid this environment, the role of school leaders has vastly changed. Schools' subjection to ever-increasing forms of external and public accountabilities mean, on the one hand, that principals and head teachers are under greater surveillance than ever before (and are especially accountable to raising the performance of underachieving and disadvantaged students), while, at the same time, schools are more self-managing and autonomous in terms of the devolution of roles that were formerly the responsibility of the state. These tensions are significant in shaping how equity is articulated in schools. They illuminate the moral imperatives of equity work and the significant role school leadership plays in such work. It is clear that the norms and values of leadership shape the way schools approach issues of equity that can, in turn, generate transformative political effects (Niesche and Keddie, 2011; Keddie and Niesche, 2012). The equity work of school leaders in the contemporary educational environment is incredibly complex, challenging and demanding. While the number of studies exploring these issues has increased in recent times, we feel there needs to be a richer theoretical engagement, focus and depth to capture this complexity. This book draws upon Foucault's work to consider the moral and ethical complexity of work undertaken in the name of social justice and equity in disadvantaged, diverse contexts.

Our aim in this book is not to search for what best leadership practice is, nor to prescribe what a specific socially just perspective must be in schools, but rather to understand and engage with the messy interplay of a range of forces that come together in this enacting, practising and working of educational leadership. Given the vast differences between and within school contexts, to prescribe ideological norms and broad perspectives for social and school change is problematic. Our approach makes transparent the ethical work that these leaders conduct on themselves towards creating schools that can address ever new and changing equity challenges. It illuminates and enables critical analysis of the moral imperatives shaping the equity work of school leaders and, in particular, the possibilities for transformative and socially just leadership that can work to dismantle some of the economic, cultural and political barriers impeding the educational success of marginalised and disadvantaged students. We argue that the complex, contradictory and messy reality of school leaders working in disadvantaged contexts requires a similarly complex toolkit of ideas in order to understand school leadership and equity practices in action.

Central to the work we undertake in this book are considerations of the purposes of education and how important the role of school leadership is in working towards these. For instance, Gert Biesta (2010) argues that the purpose of education needs to be a central and ongoing question for educational policy, practice and research. Biesta (2010: 6) further shows how the reliance on measurable outcomes, coupled with 'evidence based education', has resulted in anti-democratic education practices, a focus on managerialism and a valuing on what can be measured. These shifts towards valuing 'effectiveness' have had profound implications for educational leadership, too. Michael Fullan (2003) argues that what is needed are school leaders who have moral purpose at the centre of their leadership philosophy.

However, it is important to note that we do not align ourselves with any particular notion of 'ethical leadership' or even necessarily with approaches such as 'authentic leadership'. We, more so, emphasise leadership that works towards goals of social justice. We theorise the practices of the leaders in the case study schools, drawing on Foucault's work on ethics, power and subjectivity and his ideas of advocacy, truth-telling and counter-conduct. We illustrate how these tools can support leaders to work in socially just ways – ways that pursue both the private (academically focused) and public (socially focused) goals of schooling. For us, socially just leadership must be more than focused on improving academic results; it must be about removing the barriers and structures (be they economic, cultural or political) that constrain students' lives and their capacity to participate in the social world on a par with others (see Fraser, 2009).

This book seeks to demonstrate explicitly the usefulness of Foucault's work for thinking about leadership and school leaders' work for social justice by making sense of the ways in which leaders come to be particular subjects through these processes and discourses. We are aware of the tensions between Foucault's work and the particular understandings of social justice and alleviating inequality that have been put forward by more normative frames (for example, Nancy Fraser's three-dimensional model of justice; see Fraser, 2009). Foucault's work has been criticised as lacking a normative base in determining the differences in acceptable and unacceptable forms of power (see Fraser, 1999). We are also aware of the long history of research in the field of education that draws on a broad array of perspectives to address social justice issues. For example, issues of race, ethnicity, gender, sexuality, ability and socio-economic status have all been identified as key markers of discrimination and marginalisation of educational experiences and outcomes (Ball, 2003; Gerwitz et al., 1995; Gillborn, 2008; Keddie, 2012; Kenway et al., 1998).

Using Foucault's work, and other post-structural ideas, is often seen to be in tension with the notion of social justice for he was very much against offering normative understanding and solutions to problems. His critics have charged his work with being relativistic, self-indulgent, lacking in a normative base (Habermas, 1987; Fraser, 1999) and even reinscribing of conservative sets of power relations in the form of neoliberalism (Behrent, 2009). We are not arguing that Foucault's work tells us all there is to know about education, power and social justice. However, we feel it seeks to show how historically knowledge is intimately linked to power, and that subjects are understood as being constituted through discourse in a way that is not pre-existing and continuous. This allows an understanding of how leaders are understood in terms of constraints and possibilities for action, to constitute themselves differently as they work towards aims of social justice (see Youdell, 2006).

A useful way of helping to explain the approach used in the book is through the notion of non-normative critique (Hanson, 2014; Triantafillou, 2012). Hansen draws upon the work of Foucault and the pragmatic sociology of Boltanski to argue that non-normative critique is required to be able to abstain from any normative judgement in order to re-politicise the modes of governing and power relations, to make them contestable, to develop an openness at the level of analysis and to refuse to take up the role of reform designer (Triantafillou, 2012) or prescriber of solutions (see Foucault, 2002). We understand the difficulty of maintaining such a position in relation to social justice, but feel it is an important one in order to acknowledge that there is no essential position of truth aside from that of 'otherness' (Hanson, 2014: 13), and that 'analyses and conceptual developments can never rest on sure ground but must, like the critical operations of actors, continuously adapt to the evolutions of modes of governing' (Hansen, 2014: 15). This is a helpful way of looking at the ongoing changes in subject position brought about by the leaders in the case study schools presented later in the book, and a demonstration of how subjectivities are intimately tied to power and these different modes of governing.

We purposefully use the word 'ethics' throughout this book but not in the sense that it has often been used in the leadership and indeed educational leadership fields. We acknowledge the work done in terms of such concepts as ethical leadership and authentic leadership. However, we situate our conceptualisation of ethics drawing on Foucault's work and, as such, use the term very differently. As we explain in Chapter 3, and at length through the case study chapters (4–7), ethics refers to those ways individuals work on the self in pursuit of a particular telos or ideal self/being. In drawing on particular notions of power and formation of the self we are not seeking to identify, valorise or normalise particular ethical understandings as forms of best practice or as the most suitable for schools. Rather, we illustrate how these leaders constitute themselves as ethical subjects and how they are also constituted by certain discourses as ethical subjects as they work towards goals of social justice in their schools.

It is important to point out that throughout this book we are referring to ourselves as 'we', a common authorial voice. However, this book has come about after four years of researching and writing together. It is a culmination of a number of years of separate and common research, and the chapters consist of certain voices taking dominance while at the same time presenting a common view. For readers not familiar with our previous research, Amanda's work has focused on the broad gamut of schooling processes, practices and conditions that can impact on the pursuit of social justice in schools, including student identities, teacher identities, pedagogy, curriculum, leadership, school structures, policy agendas and socio-political trends. She has analysed these processes, practices and conditions through critical, post-structural and post-colonial lenses. Richard's research has been concerned with drawing upon post-structuralist concepts and ideas to try to theorise leadership in a different way from traditional and common approaches. Some of that previous work is found in small sections throughout this volume, but overall the book presents a bringing together of these ideas in new empirical studies with a specific focus on particular concepts from Foucault's work.

The data presented in the book represent voices from two different but similarly focused research studies. They are case studies that were conducted in Australia and England. The Australian case study focused on the practices of one leader, 'Carol', in a suburban government school in Queensland, 'Ridgeway'. The English case study focused on an alliance of schools in London, led by one secondary comprehensive school, the 'Clementine' Academy. Although the focus in each study was on socially just leadership, the different policy and social contexts of the studies and the different schools within them led to different emphases. The first study's focus is on the dynamics of leadership within a school connected closely to departmental state governance and also a new direct agreement with the federal government, but more so on the needs of a highly disadvantaged school and community. The second case study focused on leadership relations within an alliance of schools, many of which are 'academies' (i.e. schools that are granted flexibility and autonomy from local governance). As such, policies and practice associated with the intersections of school autonomy, school collaboration and accountability are emphasised in our analysis of leadership in this second case study.

The two case studies share similarities in relation to how they are situated within broader social and political contexts, but there are also dissonances. We detail these in the next and subsequent chapters as they are relevant to the case studies. While we do recognise the contextual specificities and nuances of each of the cases, the social justice lenses of the book bring the studies together. The theoretical tools we utilise to analyse the social justice capacities of the leadership practices in both studies enable a drawing out of the ways of leading that will be significant for schools (within and beyond Australia and the UK) in effectively navigating the complex and difficult terrain associated with the demands of the current climate. Rather than presenting these studies in any depth here, we explain their processes and contexts in the relevant 'data chapters' (Chapters 4 and 6). Bringing this work together under a new theoretical umbrella was, for us, a challenging but rewarding undertaking, and we feel that the end result makes a strong contribution to a field that can, at times, seem tired and lacking in fresh perspectives.

We believe that the use of Foucault, and empirical case studies from the UK and Australia, with the focus on ethical practice and schooling and leadership for social justice, facilitates an interesting and exciting take on a field that desperately needs new voices and new approaches. We are not presenting the two case studies as sites of exemplary practice, but rather use them to highlight some of the tensions for leaders and others in the contemporary moment, highly characterised by neoliberal forms of government rationality, and how they work towards improving outcomes for their students amid the contemporary demands of schools. The stories and portraits of the two schools share an explicit commitment to socially just schooling and are recognised as effective in this regard within their school communities. These portraits provide significant insight into the possibilities of leadership for social justice. Our analyses are limited to the contexts of the UK and Australia. However, the interest for other contexts will become apparent in our highlighting of the broader imperatives of education reform confronting most Western education systems in their attempts to address social justice. Our particular theorising of these issues allows for these analyses to reach beyond the specific contexts and we hope it will find resonance with readers' own education contexts. Indeed, we believe the book makes its strongest contribution in this respect. Foucault's work on ethics and especially his ideas associated with advocacy, truth-telling and counter-conduct provide fresh insights into how schools might work more productively towards greater equity for all within the demands of the current climate. They will, as we illustrate in this book, help leaders to address the multidimensionality of injustices confronting schools and education systems.

An overview of chapters

In the next chapter, we begin by foregrounding the current global education context that is still dominated by neoliberal imperatives. That is, the current climate of audit, accountabilities, managerialism, performativity and the increasing adoption of market forces into education. These discourses have had a profound effect on how leadership in education is constructed and are certainly present in our case studies. Within this section of Chapter 2 we examine each of the policy contexts as they relate to the case studies. First, we look at the state policy of Queensland as well as the federal policy background in Australia for the case study presented in Chapters 4 and 5. Then we move to the UK context and particularly the recent school reform around autonomy and collaboration to provide background for understanding the case study presented in Chapters 6 and 7. In the third section we highlight some of our concerns with the ways that leadership has been conceptualised as a part of this global movement of neoliberal accountabilities and managerialism. We argue that leadership has been compromised and that it is complicit in these neoliberal policy agendas by being constructed as the solution to many educational problems. What has ensued is a narrow, rationalist, individualist and relentless standardised drive to prescribe best leadership practice. Such an approach, we believe, not only marginalises alternative critical perspectives but serves to entrench inequality further in education provision and outcomes. We briefly explore these issues of social justice and educational leadership in the final section of the chapter.

Chapter 3 examines the theoretical tools of Michel Foucault that we draw upon to theorise and understand the case studies and leadership for social justice more broadly. We draw on Foucault's work on ethics and morality to theorise the complex micro-politics that both enable and constrain educational leaders' pursuit of economic, cultural and political justice in schools. We outline the theoretical framework that Foucault developed in his later work. We draw specifically on his fourfold frame using the notions of *ethical substance, modes of subjection, forms of elaboration* and *telos* and his ideas of advocacy, truth-telling and counter-conduct. Foucault's work on ethics is intrinsic to notions of technologies and practices of the self. We show how this notion of ethics was developed out of his earlier work on power and genealogies to provide an analysis of the subject that allows for action. The link is then made to schools and principals and how the framework can illuminate principals' subject formation and constitution as particular types of subjects in working towards their telos or ideal self.

In Chapter 4 we introduce the first of the two case studies. It focuses on a high school in Queensland, Australia (Ridgeway State

High School), and the school's principal, Carol. The school is situated in a very low socio-economic area with significant challenges relating to issues of poverty and a very diverse student population with high needs. As the principal, Carol is working towards a particular telos of leadership and social justice within this context to improve the life chances for the students. We theorise this work using Foucault's fourfold ethical framework.

We continue the analysis of Ridgeway and Carol in Chapter 5 by looking more specifically at the practices of advocacy, truth-telling and counter-conduct as key aspects of the work Carol undertakes. We consider these aspects as important for leading for social justice and not just leadership as a form of compliance to government policy and mandates. Of course, there is risk associated with these leadership practices and it is here that Carol must negotiate her way through the tricky paths of satisfying the requirements of her position while also making space for the issues she sees as important for the students and the local community.

Chapter 6 introduces the second case study. The focus is on an alliance of schools led by the Clementine Academy, a large and highly diverse secondary school located in outer London. As an 'outstanding' teaching school, Clementine heads a group of twenty schools committed to working together to improve student learning. Foucault's fourfold framework is again drawn on to articulate the ethical dimensions of Clementine's alliance leadership. The school's telos of leadership focuses on prioritising school autonomy and school collaboration, while its telos of social justice focuses on supporting all students to achieve regardless of their background circumstances.

In Chapter 7, the focus is again on notions of advocacy, truth-telling and counter-conduct as key aspects of the ethical work involved in these forms of socially just leadership. We specifically look at these notions in relation to how they promote collaboration within the Clementine-led alliance, how they foster levels of school autonomy, and how they support a sustained approach to student improvement. This analysis is not uncritical of the leadership at Clementine Academy. We illustrate the difficulty of maintaining this type of leadership practice and ethical activity within the current political climate in the UK.

In the final chapter we draw on the book's theoretical tools to bring together specific points of resonance across the two case studies. We reiterate the utility of Foucault's fourfold ethical framework in theorising leadership for social justice. We argue that the notions of truth-telling, counter-conduct and advocacy provide valuable insights into how school leaders might more effectively navigate the multifarious and uncertain terrain associated with the demands of the current climate. Despite the vastly different contextual and demographic circumstances in which school leaders might find themselves, we argue that these notions are critical in pursuing greater equity for all students.

References

Ball, S. (2003). The teacher's soul and the terrors of performativity. *Journal of Education Policy*, 18 (2), 215–228.

Behrent, M. C. (2009). Liberalism without humanism: Michel Foucault and the free market creed 1976–1979. *Modern Intellectual History*, 6, 539–568.

Biesta, G. (2010). *Good education in an age of measurement: Ethics, politics, democracy*. Boulder, CO, Paradigm Publishers.

Foucault, M. (2002). Interview with Michel Foucault. In J. D. Faubion (ed.) *Essential works of Foucault, 1954–1984*, Volume I: *Power*. London, Penguin.

Fraser, N. (1999). *Unruly practices: Power, discourse and gender in contemporary social thought*. Minneapolis, University of Minnesota Press.

Fraser, N. (2009). *Scales of justice: Re-imagining political space in a globalizing world*. New York, Columbia University Press.

Fullan, M. (2003). *The moral imperative of school leadership*. Thousand Oaks, CA, Corwin Press.

Gerwitz, S., Ball, S. J. and Bowe, R. (1995). *Markets, choice, and equity in education*. Buckingham, Open University Press.

Gillborn, D. (2008). *Racism and education: Coincidence or conspiracy?* Abingdon, Routledge.

Habermas, J. (1987). *The philosophical discourse of modernity*. Cambridge, Polity Press.

Hanson, M. P. (2014). Non-normative critique: Foucault and pragmatic sociology as tactical re-politicization. *European Journal of Social Theory* [online], 21 December, 1–19.

Keddie, A. (2012). *Educating for diversity and social justice*. New York, Routledge.

Keddie, A. and Niesche, R. (2012). Productive engagements with student difference: Supporting equity through cultural recognition. *British Educational Research Journal*, 38 (2), 333–348.

Kenway, J., Willis, S., Blackmore, J. and Rennie, J. (1998). *Answering back: Girls, boys and feminism in schools*. London, Routledge.

Lingard, R., Sellar, S. and Savage, G. (2014). Re-articulating social justice as equity in schooling policy: The effects of data and testing infrastructures. *British Journal of Sociology of Education*, 35 (5), 710–730.

Niesche, R. and Keddie, A. (2011). Foregrounding issues of equity and diversity in educational leadership. *School Leadership and Management*, 31 (1), 65–77.

Triantafillou, P. (2012). *New forms of governing: A Foucauldian inspired analysis*. Basingstoke, Palgrave Macmillan.

Youdell, D. (2006). Diversity, inequality, and a post-structural politics for education. *Discourse: Studies in the Cultural Politics of Education*, 27 (1), 33–42.

2 Contexts of educational leadership and social justice

Issues of social justice and equity have become more pronounced in the field of educational leadership in recent years. There has been particular concern with how such issues are shaped by broader neoliberal rationalities, regimes and practices, including new managerialism, high-stakes testing and accountabilities. These powerful global reforms have impacted upon issues of social justice more generally but also specifically within education. In particular, they have rearticulated social justice priorities in schools to a very narrow focus on the 'private' goals of education (namely, social efficiency and social mobility) at the expense of 'public' goals (namely, democratic and citizenship goals). As we stressed in Chapter 1, leadership in schools needs to be about more than just improving students' achievement on narrow performance measures (Fullan, 2002). If schools are to begin to remedy the growing inequities of the social world, then school leaders must 'think and act against the grain' of the existing status quo (Giroux, 2003: 6). Equally, if schools are to take seriously the link between greater social equality and enhanced well-being and peace for all (Wilkinson and Pickett, 2009), then they must contest and resist the current social arrangements that create inequities.

We believe leadership of and in education has a significant role to play in working towards greater social equity and justice. In this chapter we provide the background contextual material to the empirical studies presented in later chapters. Educational leadership – or, perhaps more appropriately, leadership of and in education – has become a vast field drawing from a wide array of knowledges, traditions and research approaches. Navigating a way through this multitude of literature is no easy task. As a result, we have been selective in the research and literature examined in this chapter, taking as our priority those factors seen to directly affect the case study schools presented in later chapters.

Global and national contexts

Since the 1980s, a neoliberal global agenda has had a powerful influence on education policy across a number of Western countries. Principles of economic rationalism have been prevalent throughout these discourses and rationalities of government, including (but not exclusively) notions of growth, marketisation, competition, choice, improvement, standardisation, meritocracy, performativity, managerialism and so on (Ball, 2008; Grimaldi, 2012; Rizvi and Lingard, 2010). These discourses have had a profound effect on the educational systems of many countries and particularly those of England and Australia, from which the case studies in later chapters are drawn. These globalised educational policy discourses (Rizvi and Lingard, 2010) have been characterised by Sahlberg (2011) as the Global Education Reform Movement (GERM), by Ball (2008) as a generic global policy ensemble and, more specific to the leadership field, by Gunter et al. (2013) as the Transnational Leadership Package (TLP). However they might be described, what is interesting about this agenda is the maintaining of equity and social justice imperatives within these policy discourses, even though the forms of economic rationalism underpinning them appear to work against these imperatives. A prudent example of this is the prevalence of 'gap talk' within Western education contexts and the accompanying policy agendas focused on raising the educational attainment of disadvantaged students to be more in line with their 'mainstream' peers. While this focus is a major equity platform in education policy across the West (as we mention later in relation to policies such as Barack Obama's 'Race to the Top'), reductive economic agendas have worked to thwart their progress, meaning that these policies have had very little success. Indeed, 'the gap' in academic attainment between disadvantaged and advantaged learners is widening in many Western contexts.

Such agendas, of course, are located within broader economic rationalities. 'Austerity' measures since the Global Financial Crisis, for example, are having pronounced effects on the already significant gap between rich and poor. They are further entrenching inequalities of income, health and overall life chances both within and between numerous countries. There have been a number of excellent and detailed analyses of neoliberal policy in recent years, so we will not repeat them here, other than to provide a broad overview of the key aspects of this policy agenda that frame our understanding of the Australian and English education contexts.

One of the most powerful aspects of neoliberal discourse in the education policy in many parts of the world is the significance attached to test scores as markers of excellence in national schooling systems – for example, TIMMS (Trends in International Mathematics and Science Study), PISA (Programme for International Student Assessment) and PIRLS (Progress in Reading Literacy Study) at an international level and tests such as Australia's NAPLAN (National Assessment Program – Literacy and Numeracy) at a national level. These tests exemplify the accountability mechanisms of the 'audit' culture. This culture draws on business-derived concepts of measurement and evaluation (Leys, 2003) to quantify, compare and rank schools nationally and internationally, and it is endemic in Western schooling contexts.

The seemingly ever-present moral panic about the dire state of public schooling in Western countries such as the United States, the United Kingdom and Australia (see Apple, 2010, 2013) has provided a warrant for these externally imposed public standards and accountabilities. Such accountabilities have placed enormous pressure on schools. Within this environment the measurement of a school's success depends on its production of evidence (in relation to these 'standards') that it is doing things 'efficiently' and in the 'correct' way. Akin to a business model of output representation, schools, teachers and students are reduced to a form and process that is auditable. Such auditability enables them to be efficiently measured, evaluated and governed (see Ball, 2003; Lingard, 2011). According to Stephen Ball (2003: 216), they are engaging in 'performativity', which is:

> a technology, a culture and a mode of regulation that employs judgements, comparisons and displays as means of incentive, control, attrition and change based on rewards and sanctions (both material and symbolic). The performances (of individual subjects or organizations) serve as measures of productivity or output, or displays of 'quality', or 'moments' of promotion or inspection. As such they stand for, encapsulate or represent the worth, quality or value of an individual or organization within a field of judgement.

Accountability regimes in the form of standardised tests – but also, of course, myriad other ever-increasing and rigid school-related 'quality' measures, such as teacher and principal professional standards and performance indicators (addressed in more detail in the next sections as they relate to the Australian and English contexts) – regulate schools' priorities in the current era, when performance on these measures is the central indicator of school success. This performativity is a 'new form of sociality' in education based on measurements, targets, comparisons and incentives (Ball, 2003). As many have noted, in this environment, what is measurable (e.g. academic test scores) counts and what is difficult to measure (e.g. social aspects of schooling) does not. The negative effects of such performativity are well recognised. They are seen, for example, as delimiting curriculum to focus on a narrow range of tested subjects, degrading pedagogy to a limited focus on instructional and rote learning, and reducing school and teacher value to their capacities to drive up student achievement on these subjects (see Ball, 2003; Myhill, 2006; Archer and Francis, 2007; West and Pennell, 2000; West, 2010).

This sociality has long been a salient feature of schooling. However, the governance turn associated with neoliberalism has enhanced its significance and is central to the rise of the audit culture (Power, 1997; Ozga, 2009; Lingard, 2011). This audit culture wields unmistakable political power in determining the legitimacy or otherwise of schools (Rose, 1999). It encompasses modes of regulation and surveillance that generate uncertainty and anxiety for principals and teachers because they are:

> constantly judged in different ways, by different means, according to different criteria, through different agents and agencies. There is a flow of changing demands, expectations and indicators that makes one continually accountable and constantly recorded. [Educators] become ontologically insecure: unsure whether [they] are doing enough, doing the right thing, doing as much as others, or as well as others, constantly looking to improve, to be better, to be excellent.
>
> (Ball, 2003: 220)

While principals and teachers continue to find their professional and personal values challenged and displaced within this environment of hyper-regulation and accountability, these reform technologies have, in many ways, become taken for granted in schools (Ball, 2003; Apple, 2005). Indeed, such 'mechanisms of projection' (i.e. reflective of external contingencies) are so embedded in the culture of schools that they define the nature of contemporary schooling and what it means to be an educator (Bernstein, 2000; Ball, 2003). For many school leaders and teachers, however, especially within schools that serve disadvantaged communities, these mechanisms remain highly disempowering – not least because they are often mobilised in punitive ways, operating within a climate of mistrust that accuses or blames principals and teachers for students' poor academic performance (Power, 1997; Apple, 2005; Lingard, 2011).

Much of this shift in the governance of schools occurred during the 1980s and 1990s in tandem with moves to increase school autonomy. School autonomy is another powerful global education discourse that has seen radical transformation of education systems in contexts such as England, the United States and Australia (OECD, 2014; Glatter, 2012;

Smyth, 2011). Granting schools more control, authority and flexibility in relation to governance aims to generate more effective, responsive and innovative education systems. School autonomy is a form of restructuring that acts as a policy-steering mechanism by a process of the decentralisation of decision-making away from the centralised distribution of resources to one where schools are given more autonomy to make certain decisions (Caldwell, 2005). However, these systems typically still require forms of central authority, and this uneasy mix of centralisation and decentralisation can prove difficult for schools and particularly school leaders to negotiate. There are also quite large variances between and within countries as to the extent of devolution. School autonomy is also constantly rearticulated over time in changing political contexts (see Lingard et al., 2002). For example, in the Australian system, the state of Victoria was one of the earliest adopters of 'school-based management' and also undertook a much more autonomous approach for schools than other states, such as New South Wales. Recently, there has been renewed interest in school autonomy reform in Australia at both federal and state level, particularly with the instating of the Independent Public Schools (IPS) initiative across the public school systems in Western Australia and Queensland.

While political commitment to the idea of autonomous schooling is strong, there remains long-held resistance to this reform. A key criticism here is the de-emphasised role of the state – in devolving responsibility for school improvement away from the state to schools, the state can attribute liability and blame for a lack of improvement to individuals, families and communities (see Lingard and Sellar, 2012; Exley and Ball, 2011). The strongest argument against this reform, however, lies in the lack of conclusive evidence to link autonomous schooling with raising educational attainment. Whether one refers to the charter schooling litera-ture in the United States, the research into academies and free schools in England or studies concerning school-based management in Australia, granting schools greater autonomy cannot be directly associated with school improvement.

Many attribute this lack of 'success' to the market ideologies that have imbued the governance of autonomous schools (see Dingerson et al., 2008; Fabricant and Fine, 2012; Lipman, 2011). As Ravitch (2010: 227) argues, 'the market [might] serve us well when we want to buy a new car' but it is 'not the best way to deliver public services' like education. A key concern here is how the market ideals of competition and choice have played out within autonomous schools and education systems. In theory, greater competition between schools (especially encouraged with the public availability of performance data) is supposed to lead to enhanced performance, increased innovation, greater responsiveness to 'consumers' (i.e. parents' and students' needs) and a greater diversity of schools (see Dingerson et al., 2008). In practice, however, competition between schools for their 'market share' of students has tended not to enhance performance and innovation but rather to generate greater segregation and stratification within education systems. Under such conditions, especially with ever-increasing auditing and public account-abilities, inequities have been reproduced. There has, for example, been an intensifying of the gap between schools serving the privileged and those serving the underprivileged. This is reflected in a residualisation within the system, with negative consequences for students living in low socio-economic status (SES) areas (Smyth, 2011; Lamb, 2007). As Lamb's (2007) work in the state of Victoria reveals, such reforms have led to much lower enrolments in schools serving the poor, which are also left to cope with much higher concentrations of the various groups of disadvan-taged students. Within this system, particular establishments, such as small schools, primary schools and schools serving marginalised students (i.e. those that receive less funding on the basis of student numbers, those that do not have sufficient leadership density to improve their school performance and those with students who require greater material and human resource support than the norm) tend to be disadvantaged.

Such stratification in contexts such as Australia, England and the United States has highlighted inherent problems with the notion of choice with particular implications for equity (see Dingerson et al., 2008; Gunter, 2012). There are assumptions that parents can make an authen-tic choice about the quality or otherwise of their local school, but it is privileged parents and students who win out in this system. As Smyth (2011: 105) points out: 'Educational "choice", the heart of the SMS [self-managing schools], has certainly worked extremely well for savvy, upwardly mobile, middle-class educational consumers, who know how to work their schools politically to their advantage.'

School autonomy continues to be a divisive and contentious reform with proponents acclaiming its advantages and opponents decrying its disadvantages. What can be said is that it is not a magic bullet for school improvement and that it can be taken up in both productive and unproductive ways (see Glatter, 2012; Keddie, 2014). It is important to point out here that these changes to the structuring of education in countries such as the United States, England and Australia have aligned with, been amenable to and thus co-opted by agendas of privatisation and the imperatives of the market.

Against this backdrop, there has been a rearticulation of the purposes of schooling away from public goals and towards an emphasis on private benefit. We agree with Cranston et al. (2010) that both private and public goals are imperative for schools to work in socially just ways. In terms of private goals, these purposes might be defined as: social efficiency ('which is about preparing young people to be competent and productive workers'); and social mobility ('which is about providing individuals with a credential which will advantage them in the competition for desirable social positions'). In terms of public goals, these purposes might be defined as: democratic quality ('which is about preparing all young people to be active and competent citizens') (Cranston et al., 2010: 520); and equity (which is about challenging and transforming the injustices of the existing status quo) (Giroux, 2003).

Significantly for us in this book, it is important to consider the role of school leadership in these processes. Leadership can play an active role in articulating goals that do not simply comply with broader performative measures, but engage with these measures in ways that do not compromise public goals. It is within this view of schooling that we situate our approach to ethics, leadership and social justice. In the following sections we describe and analyse the relevant contexts for our case studies in setting up the later analysis of how these particular schools and leaders are working towards goals of social justice. There are distinct resonances in the social and political backdrop shaping how we represent the case study schools featured in subsequent chapters. The following two sections acknowledge this, but they are delimited to highlight the relevant Australian and English policy discourses particular to each case study and necessary to locate and understand their different leadership foci and issues. This means we do not explore many issues that are significant to social justice and leadership below. For example, we do not cover in any depth matters of Indigenous disadvantage in the Australian schooling system or matters of racial injustice within the English system. In keeping with the matters Carol raised in the first case study of Ridgeway State High School, we focus on recent Australian federal and state policy in terms of educational accountability, leadership and moves towards school-based management as well as issues relating to poverty and student underperformance. In keeping with matters raised by leaders in the second case study of the Clementine-led alliance, we focus, first, on school autonomy and specifically English policy associated with the academies programme and, second, school collaboration and English policy associated with school networks.

The Australian context

Education and schooling in Australia are constitutionally the responsibility of the states and territories. However, over the last few decades there have been varying degrees of intervention by the federal government into education policy and schooling, culminating with the extensive nationalism of schools and education by the Rudd government, elected in 2007.

During the Howard government years, between 1996 to 2007, explicitly neoliberal approaches to education and its funding were promoted to the extent that the decline in funding for government schools accelerated to make way for the creation of a market for schooling, with 'choice' and 'competition' as the mantras behind these moves. With the election of the Rudd/Gillard government in 2007, the Australian federal government embarked on what it called the 'Education Revolution'. Part of this consisted of a multi-billion-dollar school infrastructure-building programme that was also a part of the government's response to the Global Financial Crisis. The other part of the government's policy agenda was a new nationalisation programme, including a national curriculum, the National Partnership Agreements between the federal and state governments, and new accountability frameworks based on NAPLAN and the *MySchool* website. The language of this policy ensemble was couched in social democracy through reference to issues of equity and social justice, but in reality it was a localised version of neoliberal policy discourses (Lingard, 2010; 2011).

Accountabilities for this national schooling agenda primarily resided in the NAPLAN testing regime and its accompanying *MySchool* website. The introduction of the website at the start of 2010 officially signalled the open message of high-stakes testing as the prime steering mechanism of school systems in Australia (Lingard, 2010; Rizvi and Lingard, 2010). Developed by the Australian Curriculum, Assessment and Reporting Authority (ACARA), it is designed to list all schools' performance data from the National Assessment Program – Literacy and Numeracy (NAPLAN) publicly. NAPLAN testing occurs in all Australian schools in Years 3, 5, 7 and 9. These data are then benchmarked against national averages and against a number of 'like schools' throughout the country. The 'like schools' measure is a scale that is based upon socio-economic status and other measures. In addition, the second iteration of the website includes schools' financial data. Opposition to *MySchool* has come from unions and other professional education bodies primarily aimed at critiquing the validity of the data, the negative effects on pedagogy and curriculum, the development of subsequent league tables, and the naming and shaming of poorly performing schools (Hardy and Boyle, 2011; Lingard, 2010; Wu, 2010). Additionally, extraordinary attention has been paid to the website, especially in terms of tactics such as media manipulation, including the packaging of government policy for public perception and consumption. This focus on rhetoric and spin are symptomatic of governmentality in action (Gillies, 2008). The *MySchool* website, while a controversial form of governmentality, has been embraced by parents and other groups in terms of holding schools to account for their performance. It has also been welcomed in terms of the federal government's agenda to target resources to underperforming schools, for example via the National Partnership Agreements.

The National Partnership Agreements between the national government and the states and territories (subsequently discontinued) have comprised another aspect of the federal government's agenda. Specific targeted areas for these agreements include Literacy and Numeracy, Teacher Quality and Low SES Schools. Under the *National Partnership Agreement for Low Socio-Economic Status Schools* (COAG, 2009), schools become national partner schools based on their socio-economic data. Under this agreement (in the Queensland context), principals must outline specific strategies to improve performance against their own school data and also state government data. Principals are offered performance pay of an additional amount per year and a further payment if NAPLAN targets are met after three years. Principals are also often on a rolling cycle of six-month contracts, with their performance reviewed and the potential for their position to be terminated with four weeks' notice, whereupon they would be relocated to a similar-sized school elsewhere. As an added incentive under these agreements, principals are given more direct control over the hiring of their staff. The Low SES National Partnership Agreement outlines the following six priority reform areas:

- incentives to attract high-performing principals and teachers;
- adoption of best-practice performance management and staffing arrangements that articulate a clear role for principals;
- school operational arrangements that encourage innovation and flexibility;
- the provision of innovative and tailored learning opportunities;
- strengthened school accountability; and
- external partnerships with parents, other schools, businesses and communities and the provision of access to extended services.

(COAG, 2009)

The above agreement, in conjunction with other state-based education accountabilities and compliance expectations, including *MySchool*, is creating a complex new work environment for principals with intense forms of managerialism and high-stakes accountabilities taking centre stage. The specific policy approach for school principals has manifested in the establishment of the Australian Institute for Teaching and School Leadership (AITSL) and its focus on promoting quality teachers and a national standards agenda for teachers and principals. The *MySchool* website and its accompanying effects place principals under increasing scrutiny of the media and public as they are constituted as not only the heads of their schools but their bodies are implicitly 'caught up' in the production of knowledge and truth about schools and their educational practices and outcomes. Principals are constituted as subjects through various leadership and educational discourses, government tactics and practices of the self.

One way these regimes of truth play out for principals is in such leadership discourses and standards and competency frameworks that have been continually developed over the past few decades. The adoption of leadership standards and capabilities is a trend towards the merging of the performative (Lyotard, 1984) and the prescriptive (Gorard, 2005; Muijs, 2011) that claims to capture leadership as an easily identifiable and measurable phenomenon (Eacott, 2011; English, 2006). As a result, the educational leadership field has sought to develop characteristics, traits, behaviours and structures that can add to the performance of the system (Niesche, 2013). The form of accountability that is exercised through *MySchool* functions as a neoliberal rationality that produces new subjectivities heavily informed by business ethics, new managerialism and a type of bio-power that forms and stimulates the individual's desire for choice as a consumer (Suspitsyna, 2010). As such, educational issues and problems are to be solved by the market.

Another way in which performative discourses operate for school leaders and principals in particular is through the leadership standards framework, Leadership Matters (Education Queensland, 2006). In Queensland the Leadership Matters document has only recently been superseded by the national AITSL Principal Standard (AITSL, 2011) but for years it was the primary mechanism for assessing and capturing principal performance. Like other states in Australia, and other countries around the world, the standards movement in educational leadership in Queensland seems to be intensifying rather than dissipating as forms of accountability, performativity and attempts to 'capture' what leadership is have taken hold over recent decades. English (2000, 2003, 2006) has criticised standards documents as being based on limited empirical research and has suggested that they are, in essence, political documents that are repressive to other possibilities for conceptualising leadership in different ways from the traditional hierarchical and charismatic approaches that have dominated the field. Anderson (2001) refers to these discourses as comprising normative statements that are negotiated within particular networks of power that often go unrecognised by authors of such standards. In the Australian context, each state has had its own leadership standards documents and frameworks, but more recently there has been the introduction of the AITSL Principal Standard, which exists within this form of recentralisation of education policy and approaches. We will not unpack this standard here as we have already done so elsewhere (Niesche, 2012, 2013), but it is important to highlight that it is a key facet of the performativity at work for school principals in Australia and for the case study of Ridgeway in Chapters 4 and 5.

Coupled with this emphasis on the standards agenda is renewed interest in school autonomy in Australia at the federal and state level. This is another reform that, as noted earlier, is shaped by a market agenda and presents new challenges for school leaders. This is especially so in Queensland with the introduction of the Independent Public Schools (IPS) initiative in 2013 (which draws on the IPS model in Western Australia, introduced in 2010). In line with the broader rationale for autonomous schooling outlined earlier, the IPS aims to grant Queensland schools the flexibility, control and authority in governance requisite to generating more effective, responsive and innovative education systems. While devolution in Queensland, as throughout Australia, is far from new and is not explored in our Australian case study chapters, it is important to mention here that the leadership matters we examine in these chapters are significant and relevant to contemplate in relation to this reform. As recent IPS research in Western Australia illustrates, strong and well-supported educative leadership is crucial to the successful take-up of school autonomy (Melbourne University, 2013). Successfully led autonomous schools, consistent with our earlier arguments, will engage with a broad view of the purposes of schooling in relation to pursuing public and private goals.

In the Australian context, the underperformance of low SES and disadvantaged groups of students on national tests continues to be an enduring problem for education. The Organisation for Economic Cooperation and Development (OECD, 2007) has identified the links between socio-economic background and educational outcomes as being stronger in Australia than they are in many other comparable countries. The correlations between student economic and social marginality, their lower scores on standardised tests, their early school leaving ages and their future economic and social disadvantages are well recognised across Western schooling contexts. This is particularly evident in how education determines employment credentialing and students' subsequent access to the labour market (Connell, 1994; Gale and Densmore, 2000; Mills and Gale, 2010). In this way, schools tend to reinscribe class injustices. Schools are embedded within and constrained/enabled by the economic systems of their societies; they cannot by themselves overcome poverty and economic inequity. They can, however, support a more equitable distribution of material benefits (Keddie, 2012).

The challenge for schools lies in assisting marginalised students to negotiate, navigate and work through and within a system that privileges a 'cultural capital' that is white and middle class. Necessary here is providing marginalised students with access to this capital, especially through teaching them the academic skills and competencies required to enable 'success' in mainstream societies (Mills and Gale, 2010; Gerwitz et al., 1995). A key platform of socially just schooling must be to prepare these students for their future productive participation within these discourses. This means exposing them 'to the cultural capital of the dominant' in ways that do not 'close the door of their chances of "success" in society' (Mills and Gale, 2010: 83).

For Sarra (2003), crucial here is assisting marginalised students to achieve on the 'same measuring sticks' of educational achievement as their more privileged counterparts so that they can 'mix it with anybody' and 'eventually access society in the same way that any other [student] would'. In relation to issues of standardised testing, Ladson-Billings (1995: 475) similarly argues:

> as their meaning in the real world [more than ever before] serves to rank and characterise both schools and individuals . . . [it is still the case that] no matter how good a fit develops between home and school culture, students must achieve. No theory of pedagogy can escape this reality.

On this issue, Sarra (2003) questions culturally responsive teaching that undermines a focus on high academic outcomes for marginalised students. He contends that such teaching has led to a 'watering down' (or creation of separate measures) of achievement for these students, which in turn has led to their further educational and social disadvantage (see McConaghy, 2000; Antrop-González and De Jesús, 2006; Williamson and Dalal, 2007). This watering down is associated with a positioning of marginalised students along deficit lines where poor academic achievement is attributed to cultural lack rather than to broader factors, such as school and teacher practice (Knight, 1994; Chubbuck, 2010). Such a positioning, along with the low expectations, degraded pedagogy and poor educational outcomes that generally follow, is commonplace in mainstream education settings (see Russell, 2005; Banks and Banks, 2010; Ladson-Billings and Gillborn, 2004; Mills and Gale, 2010).

Within these deficit constructions there is an underlying assumption of cultural incommensurability where academic achievement is understood as incommensurable or incompatible with marginalised student culture (McConaghy, 2000). Ladson-Billings (1995: 479) argues that exemplary teachers of these students believe that they are capable of academic success and they do not permit them to choose failure in their classrooms – 'they cajole, nag, pester and bribe students to work at high intellectual levels. Absent from their discourse about students is the "language of lacking"' where marginalised student culture is aligned with 'negative characteristics' seen to be incommensurable with academic success.

It is clear that efforts within schools to be culturally responsive should not be at the expense of academic rigour, and thus should not compromise students' academic achievement. The latter is crucial to pursuing social justice and to fostering students' future access to the material benefits of society. Antrop-González and De Jesús (2006) advance a theory of critical care to represent the importance of this combination of social support and high expectations. Within this theory, high-quality interpersonal relationships (which are non-authoritarian, trusting and mutually respectful) are combined with high academic expectations (expressed through patient investments of time and the creation of reciprocal obligations between students and teachers). Such environments are especially important in challenging and transforming the deficit constructions of marginalised students that reinscribe these students' disadvantage (see also Keddie, 2012).

Attempts to tackle such disadvantage in the Australian context have recognised the significance of quality teaching and learning. The individual classroom teacher is the central player in this recognition, but this also requires various levels of support and intervention that go beyond the 'blame the teacher' syndrome that permeates many popular media reports on education. This includes recognition of the complexities of teaching in, for example, remote and rural contexts (Cape York Institute, 2007) coupled with the high turnover of teachers in such settings (Heslop, 2003), the largely white, middle-class Anglo backgrounds of teachers (Allard and Santoro, 2004), and the needs of principals in supporting teachers particularly in remote areas (Jorgensen and Niesche, 2011).

Stemming from this need, the highly influential notion of productive pedagogies arose from a longitudinal study into schooling in Queensland (Lingard et al., 2001). Productive pedagogies refer to classroom practices considered most likely to lead to improved academic performance and social learning of students. While based on the work of Newmann and associates (1996) and Newmann et al. (1995), productive pedagogies have been drawn upon in a number of research projects and studies (e.g. Allen, 2003; Hayes et al., 2006; Jorgensen et al., 2010; Keddie and Mills, 2007; Lingard et al., 2003; Munns, 2007). The productive pedagogies model consists of four main dimensions: intellectual quality; connectedness; supportive classroom environment; and valuing difference. These pedagogies are concerned with achieving better outcomes for all students through an emphasis on intellectual demand. With the introduction of high-stakes testing in Australia in the form of NAPLAN and the Masters report into education in Queensland (Masters, 2009), the emphasis has shifted away from productive pedagogies to one of preparation for tests and reform of the school system towards Independent Public Schools.

Another aspect of the Queensland longitudinal study was the development of productive leadership (Hayes et al., 2004; Lingard et al., 2003) that was centred on the work of school leaders in support of productive pedagogies and high-quality, intellectually demanding curricula. We have drawn upon this idea in previous research (see Niesche and Keddie, 2011) and we build on this work here in offering further insight into how school principals can work to address issues of equity and educational outcomes. In the next section we move to an examination of the context in England.

The English context

Neoliberal and neo-conservative ideologies have made an indelible impact on education policy in England since the 1980s. These market-oriented ideologies have been particularly salient in relation to matters of school autonomy and accountability (see Bradley and Taylor, 2010; Glatter, 2012; Lawson et al., 2013; Ball, 2003). On the one hand, educational reform has instated greater powers to schools with the dismantling of local (local authority) governance and greater direct resourcing to schools. State support for the establishment of a vast array of school model options variously funded through government, private industry and charity support has opened up and diversified the education system. These reforms are undergirded by the premise referred to earlier: that greater school autonomy, diversity and choice will encourage innovation and quality teaching and drive up school performance (DfE, 2010; Chapman and Salokangas, 2012; Lupton, 2011).

On the other hand, as with Australian education, reform in England has instated a prescriptive national curriculum and assessment framework where student performance on key stage tests is audited and converted to a public ranking of schools in the form of league tables. School 'effectiveness' is additionally policed and regulated through Ofsted (Office for Standards in Education) inspections (Glatter, 2012; Lawson et al., 2013; Boyle and Charles, 2011). These external forms of accountability have become increasingly 'high stakes', given that a school's reputation is based on its performance on these measures. Such performance is seen to encapsulate a school's effectiveness, worth and value (Ball, 2003). The increasing emphasis on global measures of school effectiveness – that is, the nation's performance on international testing regimes, such as those mentioned earlier (e.g. PISA and TIMMS) – has worked to validate these forms of accountability in England (as indeed they have in Australia). International auditing and the desire to be 'world class' and to 'succeed' on a global scale have strengthened the warrant for the current forms of accountability and auditing that characterise school reform in England (Boyle and Charles, 2011; Bhattacharya, 2013).

The combination of autonomy and accountability reform in England has transformed this school system from one ostensibly based on equal provision through state management and allocation to one based on an incentive structure geared towards maximising levels of funding and outputs in terms of students' test and examination results (see West and Bailey, 2013; Lingard and Sellar, 2012; West and Pennell, 2000; Gunter, 2012; Bhattacharya, 2013; Bradley and Taylor, 2010). Ball and Junemann (2012) define the transformation of English schooling as a disarticulation of state education. They describe the new administrative structure as reflecting a 'heterarchical' rather than hierarchical system of relations that is increasingly complex in its overlap, multiplicity and asymmetric power dynamics. Such disarticulation has generated a new style of governance that involves a proliferation of new players – or stakeholders – who are now responsible for schools and schooling from state agencies, quangos and businesses to voluntary organisations, charities, philanthropic organisations and faith groups. The work of governance in this realm 'is increasingly dispersed and opaque, being done in a myriad of policy microspaces' (Ball and Junemann, 2012: 139). For Ball and Junemann (2012), this heterarchical system is a new modality of state power undergirded by the values of meritocracy and enterprise. While it reflects greater intertwining, blurring and instability of powers in the processes of governance, the 'core executive' of the state retains substantial authority and public presence within policy.

While the neoliberal ideologies underpinning such transformation resonate somewhat with previous 'Third Way' education reforms under New Labour, reforms of this ilk have been radically and rapidly escalated since 2010 with the governing coalition's 'Big Society' platform and its mandate of 'empowering' local people and communities. It is a new game of school leadership based on an accelerated competitive marketisation (Gunter, 2012) and a 'renewed emphasis on civil society as the primary locus of response to social problems, rather than state intervention' (Lingard and Sellar, 2012: 48). Responsibility for school improvement in this climate has shifted from a state to a non-state matter. While, to be sure, state intervention to support school improvement still exists, the responsibility for school improvement is seen as the domain of the school, local community, family or individual. However, what constitutes school improvement remains firmly within the province of state authority and clearly rests on the capacity of schools to raise standards on particular performance indicators (see Exley and Ball, 2011; Ball and Junemann, 2012).

Such shifts, consistent with the research presented earlier, have amplified competition between schools within the English education system in ways that privilege particular schools while marginalising others. In this environment, 'good' schools (i.e. those that raise standards on tests and exams) have flourished while 'bad' schools (i.e. those that do not do well) have not. Small schools and schools serving marginalised and disadvantaged students have not fared well. Their demographics and circumstances mean that it is impossible for them to compete with more privileged schools and to live up to the narrow performative demands of the audit culture (Ball, 2003; Glatter, 2012; West and Ylönen, 2010). Such competition has increased segregation between schools and the hierarchical ordering or '"tiering" that is already a sharp feature of the system – accentuating stratification based on social factors and academic ability' (Glatter, 2012: 565; see also Bradley and Taylor, 2010; Lupton, 2011).

As in other Western contexts, there are major concerns in England about how these shifts have rearticulated what constitutes 'quality' teachers and teaching. As noted earlier, the standards and audit culture is seen as impoverishing the curriculum in skewing it towards the metric of tested subjects and degrading pedagogy to a 'one-size-fits-all' delivery model. As many commentators have argued, the government's preoccupation with raising achievement on (narrowly conceived) academic tests has resulted in a situation where 'quick-fix' strategies to produce short-term gains in 'test scores' overrule the learning agenda (see Myhill, 2006; Archer and Francis, 2007). In this regard, standardised tests have become the raison d'être of teaching, the benchmark of school success or failure (De Waal, 2006). This focus is seen as not only reducing teaching to a 'banking' or knowledge transfer model but also as side-lining the moral and social purposes of schooling (especially evident, for example, in downgrading the importance of subject areas such as Citizenship and PSHE (Personal, Social and Health Education) that focus on these purposes).

In line with these rearticulations, there has been a marked shift away (especially in England, relative to other parts of the UK) from the notion of teaching as a research-based profession and towards a re-emphasis on 'practicality' and 'relevance' (Beauchamp et al., 2013). Privileged in current versions of teacher standards and current models of teacher 'education' (or 'training', as it is now more usually known) is 'practical' and experiential knowledge over theoretical, pedagogical and subject knowledge (Beauchamp et al., 2013). In relation to teacher standards, the current performative emphasis around narrow and prescriptive measures of teacher and school effectiveness has prioritised a focus on teachers' 'behaviour, rather than on their intellectuality' (Evans, 2011: 851). In relation to initial teacher education, this emphasis has delimited curriculum to include very little focus on the education disciplines of history, philosophy, psychology and sociology (Beauchamp et al., 2013). Consistent with these shifts in understanding teacher quality around 'practicality' and 'relevance' has been the policy agenda to transfer control for teacher training from universities to schools (DfE, 2010). McNamara (2013) notes that successive governments of all political persuasions in England since 1984 have legislated to make teacher training more focused on the 'practical' knowledge of teaching. However, the introduction of programmes such as Schools Direct (by the current coalition government) is providing the architecture to realise an ideologically driven understanding of teaching as essentially a 'craft' or a set of skills that can be prescribed, quantified and evaluated, rather than a complex, contextual and intellectual activity. Schools Direct, established in 2011, is a classroom-based training route for teachers in which graduates largely 'learn on the job' rather than in university classrooms. It is not only interfering with the equitable distribution of new teachers across the system but has been accused of 'choking off' the best teacher training courses and driving them out of business (see Bell, 2015).

The 'academies' movement has been a major reform amid these changes. This exemplifies the political logic of the coalition's Big Society agenda of empowerment, on the one hand, and competitive marketisation, on the other. Similar to self-managing schools in Australia or charter schools in the United States, academies are independent, non-fee-paying state schools. They operate as charities, with their revenue costs remaining largely covered by the state alongside some financial contributions from non-government donors, including entrepreneurs, charities, businesses, faith groups and universities (see Ball, 2009; Pennell and West, 2009; Glatter, 2012). The policy goals of academisation include increasing school diversity and parental choice and, via competition and freedom from local governance, improving educational standards and innovation (see West and Bailey, 2013; Wilkins, 2012).

Of course, attempts to increase school autonomy are not new in England. The Education Reform Act of 1988, for example, enabled schools to opt out of local authority control and become 'grant maintained' – owned by charitable foundations (although this opting out was later overturned by the Schools Standards and Framework Act of 1998; see West and Bailey, 2013). Academies were introduced by the New Labour government in 2000 (a programme designed to replace failing schools in struggling areas), but their forebears were city technology colleges, introduced by a Conservative government in 1986. It was the Academies Act of 2010, however, that led to the rapid expansion and proliferation of academies because it opened up the possibility for all publicly funded schools to convert to 'academy status'. This Act led to system-wide change under the coalition government, especially by increasing the role of private bodies in the delivery of school-based education. The academies movement is a mechanism that sits within the shift in the delivery of school-based education from public bodies such as local authorities to non-government or private bodies. Consistent with the literature mentioned earlier, there are grave concerns in England with how the market ideologies governing this movement are further undermining the equity priorities of public education. Furthermore, the dismantling of local authority (democratically elected, public body) control is seen as profoundly undemocratic, while the movement's drawing away of public money to the private sector is seen, among other things, as likely to privilege the interests of business and enterprise over educative goals (see West and Bailey, 2013).

In England, more than half of all secondary schools have now converted to academy status. Academy status gives schools freedom from the control of the local authority and has, in most cases (although to varying extents), resulted in schools receiving greater direct funding (money that would otherwise have gone to the authority to distribute to the schools under its control). Academies are granted flexibility in relation to the delivery of curriculum, the level of staff salaries and working conditions, and even the dates of the school term and duration of the school day. They also enjoy a measure of freedom in relation to their use of monies received from the Department for Education to support their disadvantaged or underprivileged learners (as part of closing the gap): for example, the funding distributed to schools as part of the Free School Meals and Pupil Premium programmes. The Free School Meals programme is a national government initiative that is available on application. It is generally allocated to children whose parents are in receipt of social welfare support and it provides a free lunchtime meal. The Pupil Premium provides extra funding to public schools for disadvantaged students, with the funding associated with students' eligibility for free school meals.

Such freedom and flexibility are, of course, strictly regulated within the high-stakes frame of broader accountability measures: for example, the Department for Education has directed many 'underperforming' schools (as designated by Ofsted evaluations) to become 'sponsored' academies. (Most other academies are 'converter' academies. These tend to be relatively high-performing schools that choose to become academies.) This means that they lose autonomy as they are placed under the direction of a sponsor (which might be a successful school, a chain of schools or a business or university), which is then held accountable for improving their performance (DfE, 2013).

Amid these policy moves to increase school autonomy, there has been increasing recognition of the significance of school-to-school networking or collaboration. While school networking in various forms has been a prominent feature of contemporary schooling in England (as elsewhere) for some time, greater school autonomy has increased the incentive for schools to collaborate (Sliwka, 2003). Indeed, for schools to succeed and flourish in the current autonomous and heterarchical environment of increasingly high-stakes accountability, they need to work with and learn from other schools in ways that have not been mainstreamed in the past (Watterston and Caldwell, 2011). This premise has underpinned the burgeoning international policy emphasis on school-to-school collaborations. There is hope that such collaborations may offer a productive alternative to 'cumbersome bureaucracies' by meeting the new demands confronting schools and education systems in offering a source of governance that is less hierarchical, more democratic and cooperative and more responsive to the specific needs of schools than centralised systems of regulation (Sliwka, 2003; Chapman et al., 2005). For Sliwka (2003: 63), they can be a 'vibrant, powerful force [of] democratic exchange and mutual stimulation and motivation'. They can be a means for capacity-building and professional development through 'the dissemination of innovative educational practices among principals and teachers in different schools'. Such collaboration is seen to be particularly important in mediating between centralised and decentralised structures and in ameliorating some of the fragmentation, disconnection and isolation engendered by autonomous schooling (Sliwka, 2003; Hargreaves, 2011).

School collaboration has been a significant focus of English education policy. Various government schemes have supported the creation of school networks in their education improvement agendas: for example, the Excellence in Cities initiative and the Leading Edge Partnership programme (see Black-Hawkins, 2007). The Network Learning Communities (NLC) programme, instated between 2002 and 2006 and funded by the National College for School Leadership, was one of the largest school improvement projects of networked professional learning and development of its time (see Sammons et al., 2007). Another initiative supporting the creation of school networks was the London Challenge (Ofsted, 2010). In this programme school networks were purported to be key drivers in lifting the performance of schools across London. Established in 2003, the aim of these networks was to audit and tailor specific human and material support to meet the specific needs of (particularly lower-performing) schools and to monitor and review the progress of these schools. Another major overarching purpose of this programme was to generate a collective sense of responsibility and commitment across schools for improving the learning outcomes of students. Similarly, the 2010 White Paper *The Importance of Teaching* (DfE, 2010) articulates the significance of professional collaboration between schools in turning the English education system into one of the world's top performers.

In policy terms, then, the expectation seems to be that school networks will play a central role of connectedness and coherence within the complexity and multiplicity of the current autonomised system.

Collaborations between schools within current educational reform are complex and assume a variety of forms. They are created for different purposes and for various reasons and thus support and network with schools in different ways. Referring to the situation in England, Hargreaves (2011) defines these networks along a 'loose-to-tight' continuum, which is suggestive of the autonomy individual schools might enjoy within a particular alliance, from the 'loose' and superficial connections that might characterise an informal collective to the 'tight' control that might characterise a 'hard federation' or chain of schools. According to Hargreaves, most clusters fall between these two extremes, but the key factors of an attractive and effective cluster for schools and their leaders are voluntary membership and flexible ties.

Such key factors are consistent with the principles of effective school collaborations outlined in other English-based research (see Muijs et al., 2011; Black-Hawkins, 2007). While acknowledging that there is no one recipe for fostering effective networking, this research delineates several important elements that support it:

- *ownership*, where partner schools, and particularly the head teachers, feel that they have reasonable control over agendas;
- commitment to a *common purpose* – that of improving teaching and learning across all schools; and
- *shared responsibility* for student learning outcomes across the group.

Collaborations based on or supporting these elements were associated in this research with improving educational outcomes through an emphasis on mutual learning, reflection and the sharing of ideas. These elements of effective networking resonate with aspects of organisational capital outlined by Hargreaves (2011) as necessary for educational leaders to lead a network successfully. Distinguishing between the organisational capital required for leading a school with that of leading a network, Hargreaves delineates five distinctive elements of partnership competence, including:

1   understanding schools as learning communities;
2   investing in teaching and learning innovation;
3   engaging in the practice of distributed leadership;
4   working with other schools in reciprocal ways; and
5   adapting local knowledge to address the distinctive needs of particular contexts.

Other research that is more specifically focused on networking programmes – such as Chapman et al.'s (2005) study of how the NLC supports schools in challenging circumstances – also highlights the significance of such elements of partnership competence.

The Department for Education in England has instated many structural reforms within the context of academisation: for example, academy federations or chains, which are governed under multi-academy and umbrella trusts. Most of these reforms recognise the significance of these aspects of school collaboration; however, evidence is emerging as to the types of collaborations that might offer the greatest scope in supporting schools to cope with the demands of the present context. It is perhaps too early to make any definitive assertions as to the efficacy or otherwise of current network reform on school improvement in England. Certainly, if the past is any guide, it is clear that productive school networks are exceedingly difficult to create and sustain; and, perhaps because of this, they have had little success (in the main) in improving student learning outcomes – shaped and constrained as they are by differing degrees of commitment, reciprocity and capacity and varying complexities of structure and process (see Hadfield, 2005; Sammons et al., 2007). The challenges of the present, more autonomised environment may exacerbate these difficulties. Consistent with the arguments against the proliferation of academies, there are concerns about the role of networks in the present system, given the dismantling of local authority control. While local authorities are democratically elected public bodies that can oversee, scrutinise and mediate central policy, networks have no such democratic imperative or mandate. Indeed, networks (whether in the form of chains, academy federations or other collaborations), given the imperatives of the audit culture, are more likely to be governed by enterprise and narrow performative goals rather than collaboration, reciprocity and support.

Academy chains have been subjected to particular criticism in this regard. The rapid expansion of some chains is seen as evidence of enterprise and economic, rather than educative, imperatives. Moreover, adhering to democratic and distributive modes of leadership and management in line with sustaining this rapid growth has proven difficult in some cases. There are also concerns about the potential loss of autonomy for individual schools under the standardised frame of some academy chains and the lack of sharing of learning expertise, knowledge and skills beyond chains (Hill, 2010; Hill et al., 2012). Another major concern with network governance of autonomous schools is the increasing involvement of new philanthropies and the for-profit sector. While not explored in this book, it is important to acknowledge the significant and growing body of research that highlights how the business priorities of these new players are undermining democratic and inclusive public school governance (see Lipman, 2011; Ball and Junemann, 2012).

More promising, according to Hill et al. (2012), are the networks currently being formed as part of the Department for Education's National Teaching Schools initiative, which is supported by the National College for Teaching and Leadership (2011). Similar to the agenda of academy chains, the National Teaching Schools initiative is focused on school improvement through collaboration and the drawing together of expertise across schools to this end. Also similar to the agenda of chains, it supports self-sustainable improvement because it is school-led and -based, with assuring the quality of the work generated through the collective the responsibility of the collective itself. Teaching schools are selected to lead an alliance of schools within this initiative on the basis that they are 'outstanding' – as evidenced by high levels of student performance and strong head teacher leadership. These schools must also have a strong track record of working collaboratively with other schools. Teaching schools provide training and support for the other schools within their alliance. They identify and coordinate expertise from the alliance to deliver such support by using the best leaders and teachers to conduct professional learning and development for newly qualified and more experienced teachers; coordinating peer-to-peer professional and leadership development; and engaging in research and development (National College for Teaching and Leadership, 2011; Hargreaves, 2011; Matthews and Berwick, 2013).

To be sure, teaching schools, like other school network initiatives, are cogs in the government's Big Society machinery, which is designed to transform the English school system from local democratic governance to devolved private management 'steered' all the while by the accountability regimes of the state (see Osborne and Gaebler, 1992). As their mandate extends to initial teacher training through Schools Direct or by gaining accreditation as an initial teacher training provider (National College for Teaching and Leadership, 2014), their role in this milieu may be all the more worrying, as we indicated earlier. In this book, we accept these concerns but nonetheless try to highlight in the English case study (in Chapters 6 and 7) how one teaching school and its network are attempting to navigate through the tensions and demands of the current climate in productive and equitable ways.

The warrant for a focus on how this reform is being mobilised in productive ways is certainly to be found in the inconclusive evidence as to the efficacy of school networking in improving student learning. While there are many accounts of school network success, there are also many of school network failure. In general, as with the shift to increasing school autonomy, such policy reform has not led to consistently improved academic outcomes (see Academies Commission, 2013; Gorard, 2009; Sammons et al., 2007).

The compromising of leadership

Effective or good leadership has increasingly been presented as the solution to many of education's pressing problems. The field is replete with best-practice scenarios and the keys to effective school leadership. This is partly understandable with the hegemonic adoption of neoliberal forms of governance and policy in many Western countries that are relying on forms of high-stakes testing, performativity, high-level accountabilities and auditing. What these forms of governance require, it has been argued, are forms of leadership that are effective and efficient in the implementation of these agendas. What have been put forward as required are forms of leadership that can work and comply with these agendas. For example, Helen Gunter (2012) has conducted a comprehensive study into the construction of the leadership industry under New Labour in England. Not only has a particular form of leadership been valorised in these accounts (for example, transformational and distributed leadership models), but the leadership industry has played no small part in putting forward particular models, ideas and standards that serve to prop up these reforms and preserve the status quo: that is, education systems characterised by high levels of inequality, such as those in England, the United States and Australia.

Similar criticisms have also emerged from other scholars on this construction and deployment of leadership as the solution to education's problems (Niesche, 2013). Pasi Sahlberg has written extensively on what he terms the Global Education Reform Movement (GERM), which involves such phenomena as the standardisation of education, the focus on core subjects such as numeracy and literacy, low-risk solutions to improve learning outcomes, extensive use of corporate management models and test-based accountability policies (Sahlberg, 2011). Implicit in Sahlberg's critique of the GERM is the role of leadership and the leadership industry's complicity in these policies. Although not in the field of education, others have also been critical of this leadership industry, which has created a problematic link between individuals and organisational outcomes (Kellerman, 2012; Lakomski, 2005). These links have been exploited by some in education, which has resulted in a weak and poor research profile for educational leadership (Gorard, 2005; Muijs, 2011). Furthermore, Nigel Wright (2001, 2011) uses the term 'bastard leadership' to refer to an approach to school leadership whereby leaders are little more than 'ciphers in the managerialist project' (Wright, 2011: 345). Wright (2011: 349) goes on to explain that

Bastard leadership, as part of a managerialist approach, was built upon central government direction and prescriptions, a regime of targets, predicated on a view which emphasised the homogeneity of schools, leading to 'one size fits all' solutions based on linear heuristics for a wide range of educational issues.

Of course, these forms of managerialism were accompanied by a strict form of compliance that continues to be a huge risk for school heads (Thomson, 2009). This can be even more starkly illustrated by the recent 'firing' of heads in England. As we show in the case study presented in Chapters 4 and 5, similar measures have formed part of the National Partnership Agreements in Australia, with school principals on short-term contracts forced to accept strict compliance responsibilities and facing the constant threat of being fired or 'moved on'.

In the foreword to a new Routledge book series on critical educational leadership, management and administration scholarship, the series editors introduce the notion of the 'transnational leadership package' (Gunter et al., 2013).[1] In using this concept Gunter, Thomson and Blackmore are referring to a convergence of Educational Leadership Management and Administration (ELMA) paradigms that is increasingly seeing a transnational field of educational research that is primarily interested in working towards the standardisation and normalisation of what constitutes good leadership through the development of leadership standards and programmes of professional development. This 'leadership industry' promotes the international circulation of best-practice models and ideas of leadership that are sold as the solutions to numerous educational problems. Gunter, Thomson and Blackmore are also quick to point out that they do not necessarily see these leadership approaches and models as a virtuous circle of activity in presenting policy anxiety and problems coupled with the appropriate solution. The rise of for-profit players in the education marketplace – what many refer to as 'edu-business' – has seen some dubious operators enter the education policy arena.

Thrupp and Willmott (2003) use the term 'textual apologists' to refer to the way that school leadership literature has been used to prop up recent managerialist reform in education (see also Thrupp, 2003). They argue that there are three categories of textual apologism – problem-solving, overt apologism and subtle apologism – that are symptomatic of the ways in which leadership is used as a tool for neoliberal education reform and are largely uncritical of leadership and the complexity of school contexts. They also use the term 'textual dissenters' to designate those who are interested in critical, alternative accounts of leadership practice. We certainly situate ourselves within this latter category in this book, as we are interested in creating different accounts of leadership for social justice, and ones that provide new insights drawing on the ethical framework and theories of Michel Foucault.

These critical approaches to educational leadership point to a compromising of leadership in the sense that particular instrumentalist notions are being put forward that are not only unrepresentative of the work that many school leaders do, but are also harmful to those same leaders when they are forced to comply with extreme managerialism and accountability measures. These discourses have also pushed other views and understandings of leadership to the periphery: for example, a range of critical perspectives, including social justice, post-structuralist ideas, feminist, anti-racist and anti-imperialist discourses. That is, those discourses that are not seen to be increasing performativity and those that do not illustrate the latest best-practice model nor how to solve specific leadership problems. Like many others, we believe leadership, as such, has been compromised by this trend. There needs to be a broader knowledge base, with more transdisciplinary ideas and different theoretical perspectives, not just a rehashing of previous models with the latest adjectival phrase. This is why we draw upon Foucault's more recent and less utilised work in relation to ethics to offer new insights and move beyond the narrow frames of what good leadership is or should be and to accord an explicit focus on issues of social justice and equity in schools. In the next section we explore some of the recent work undertaken in this area of educational leadership and social justice.

Educational leadership for social justice

In Chapter 1 we articulated our position in relation to a non-normative approach to social justice through the tools of Michel Foucault. As we stated, our position is not one of prescribing what a normative view of social justice should be, but rather outlining how school leaders are governed and govern themselves in working towards particular goals of social justice and equity. We have adopted this approach because it allows us to remain open to different forms of analysis and means we are able to analyse how individuals are constituted through particular practices and discourses. The field of educational leadership has also historically understood issues of social justice, equity, feminist and critical approaches as marginal: that is, they have been sidelined by core constructions of leadership practice according to models of best practice and efficiency (Blackmore, 2006). However, more recently, there has been increased interest in leadership for social justice with the broader recognition that not only are some groups of students performing well below others but also that schools are perpetuating and re-enforcing those inequities

(Hayes et al., 2006; Teese and Polesel, 2003). Nevertheless, despite a number of well-intentioned school reform efforts, students from low SES communities and backgrounds, and students who are not from dominant, successful, white, middle-class backgrounds, continue to underperform in schools (Shields, 2003, 2004). Increased governmental concern with 'reducing the gap' in a number of Western countries has highlighted the role of education, schools and school leadership as important vehicles for reducing inequality. Reforms such as No Child Left Behind (NCLB) and Obama's later Race to the Top initiative in the United States, Every Child Matters in the UK and the Melbourne Declaration on Educational Goals for Young Australians have all demonstrated an awareness among governments of these inequities in education systems and the risks for particular groups of students. However, as mentioned earlier, critics of NCLB and Race to the Top, for example, have argued that the emphasis on market- and test-driven reforms is only exacerbating inequities (see Darling-Hammond and Wood, 2008; Rothstein, 2004).

We also acknowledge that concepts such as leadership and social justice are discursive constructs from particular economic, political and social imperatives and as such are highly contested notions. Our view of leadership is one that sees it as a form of social relationship that 'is practised by many teachers, principals and parents in a range of educational sites and in a number of informal as well as formal administrative positions' (Blackmore, 1999: 6). Consequently, we acknowledge that leadership should be considered everyday practice, not only a characteristic of exceptional individuals. We also make the distinction that leadership is not 'everywhere' or exercised by everyone.

Leadership for social justice has been explored by a number of scholars over recent years (e.g., Blackmore, 2006, 2008, 2010; Marshall, 2004; Normore, 2008; Ryan, 2010; Shields, 2010; Theoharis, 2007, 2010). However, what has been less explored or acknowledged is the contested nature of leadership itself and its relationship with the discourses of social justice and equity. This is where the often narrow and insular knowledge base of educational leadership fails to engage with a long history of sociological, political and philosophical perspectives on issues such as social justice and equity. As a result, discourses of managing diversity and difference have been prioritised (Morrison et al., 2006; Wilkinson, 2008) while the social, economic and political dimensions of these debates have not been recognised. What can then occur is an othering of minority cultures and perspectives whereby dominant, white, Western ways of knowing and 'leading' are reinforced (see Keddie and Niesche, 2012; Niesche and Keddie, 2011).

If principals are to play a key role in addressing educational disadvantage among particular groups, then there needs to be more in-depth study and analysis of the factors and challenges that they face on the ground in schools. It is then that improved ways of working and new approaches can be developed to facilitate not only a more equitable education system but improvements in overall performance levels. These strategies need to come from the local level – that is, the school level – in order to meet the needs of the local school community in the best way possible. It has been argued approaches such as productive leadership (Hayes et al., 2004; Niesche and Keddie, 2011) and democratic styles of leadership are better suited to leadership for social justice (Blackmore, 2006; Lingard et al., 2003) and supporting teachers (Hayes et al., 2006). However, there remains a distinct lack of research detailing the day-to-day working experiences of principals undertaking this challenging work. This book aims to improve our understanding of these issues.

Conclusion

In this chapter we have started the discussion of the contextual issues that frame the theoretical approach we outline in the next chapter and the two case studies. We have described the global and national contexts that are driving education reform and also the implications of these on leaders in schools. We have argued here that one cannot divorce leadership from these broader issues, and we show in later chapters how these issues manifest and play out in the case studies in London, England, and Queensland, Australia. We have highlighted the specificities of each of the two contexts, and made the case that the notion of leadership has been compromised by these broader global factors closely tied to neoliberal modes of governance of education. Finally, we have briefly examined some of the recent work undertaken in the area of leadership and social justice to foreground the work done in this book, and we firmly situate the book within this field, albeit with a different theoretical set of concepts drawn from Foucault's work. We explore these in more detail in the next chapter.

Note

1 The first three books in this series were Gunter (2013), Gillies (2013) and Niesche (2013).

References

Academies Commission (2013). *Unleashing greatness*. London, RSA.
Allard, A., and Santoro, N. (2004). Making sense of difference? Teaching identities in postmodern contexts. Paper presented at the Australian

Association of Research in Education Conference, Melbourne, November–December.

Allen, J. (2003). Productive pedagogies and the challenge of inclusion. *British Journal of Special Education*, 30 (4), 175–179.

Anderson, G. (2001). Disciplining leaders: A critical discourse analysis of the ISLLC National Examination and Performance Standards in educational administration. *International Journal of Leadership in Education*, 4 (3), 199–216.

Antrop-González, R. and De Jesús, A. (2006). Toward a theory of critical care in urban small school reform: Examining structures and pedagogies of caring in two Latino community-based schools. *International Journal of Qualitative Studies in Education*, 19 (4), 409–433.

Apple, M. (2005). Education, markets and an audit culture. *Critical Quarterly*, 47 (1–2), 11–29.

Apple, M. (2010). *Global crises, social justice and education*. New York, Routledge.

Apple, M. (2013). *Can education change society?* New York, Routledge.

Archer, L. and Francis, B. (2007). *Understanding minority ethnic achievement: Race, gender, class and 'success'*. Abingdon, Routledge.

Australian Institute for Teaching and School Leadership (AITSL) (2011). *National professional standard for principals*. Carlton South, Victoria, Ministerial Council for Education, Early Childhood Development and Youth Affairs (MCEEDYA).

Ball, S. (2003). The teacher's soul and the terrors of performativity. *Journal of Education Policy*, 18 (2), 215–228.

Ball, S. (2008). *The education debate*. Bristol, Policy Press.

Ball, S. (2009). Academies in context: Politics, business and philanthropy and heterarchical governance. *Management in Education*, 23 (3), 100–103.

Ball, S. and Junemann, C. (2012). *Networks, new governance and education*. Bristol, Policy Press.

Banks, J. and Banks, C. (eds) (2010). *Multicultural education: Issues and perspectives*. Hoboken, NJ, John Wiley and Sons.

Beauchamp, G., Clarke, L., Hulme, M. and Murray, J. (2013). *Research and teacher education: The BERA–RSA inquiry: Policy and practice within the United Kingdom*. London, British Educational Research Association.

Bell, D. (2015). School Direct is choking university teacher-training courses. *Guardian*, 19 January. From www.theguardian.com/higher-education-network/2015/jan/19/school-direct-is-choking-university-teacher-training-courses, accessed 10 March 2015.

Bernstein, B. (2000). Official knowledge and pedagogic identities: The politics of re-contextualising. In S. Ball (ed.) *The sociology of education: Major themes*. London, Routledge Falmer.

Bhattacharya, B. (2013). Academy schools in England. *Childhood Education*, 89 (2), 94–98.

Black-Hawkins, K. (2007). Networking schools. In C. McLaughlin, K. Black-Hawkins, D. McIntyre and A. Townsend (eds) *Networking practitioner research*. Hoboken, NJ, Taylor and Francis.

Blackmore, J. (1999). *Troubling women: Feminism, leadership and educational change*. Buckingham, Open University Press.

Blackmore, J. (2006). Social justice and the study and practice of leadership in education: A feminist history. *Journal of Educational Administration and History*, 38 (2), 185–200.

Blackmore, J. (2008). Leading educational re-design to sustain socially just schools under conditions of instability. *Journal of Educational Leadership, Policy and Practice*, 23 (2), 18–33.

Blackmore, J. (2010). Preparing leaders to work with emotions in culturally diverse educational communities. *Journal of Educational Administration*, 48 (5), 642–658.

Boyle, B. and Charles, M. (2011). Education in a multicultural environment: Equity issues in teaching and learning in the school system in England. *International Studies in Sociology of Education*, 21 (4), 299–314.

Bradley, S. and Taylor, J. (2010). Diversity, choice and the quasi-market: An empirical analysis of secondary education policy in England. *Oxford Bulletin of Economics and Statistics*, 72 (1), 10–26.

Caldwell, B. (2005). *School-based management*. International Academy of Education. From https://smec.curtin.edu.au/local/documents/Edpol3.pdf, accessed 10 March 2015.

Cape York Institute (2007). *Teach for Australia: A practical plan to get great teachers into remote schools*. From www.cyi.org.au/WEBSITE%20uploads/Education%20Attachments/Teach%20For%20Australia 1.pdf, accessed 10 March 2015.

Chapman, C. and Salokangas, M. (2012). Independent state-funded schools: Some reflections on recent developments. *School Leadership and Management*, 32 (5), 473–486.

Chapman, C., Allen, T. and Harris, A. (2005). *Networked learning communities and schools facing challenging circumstances*. Warwick, University of Warwick Press.

Chubbuck, S. (2010). Individual and structural orientations in socially just teaching: Conceptualization, implementation, and collaborative effort. *Journal of Teacher Education*, 61 (3), 197–210.

Connell, R. W. (1994). Poverty and education. *Harvard Educational Review*, 642, 125–149.

Council of Australian Governments (COAG) (2009). *National partnership agreement on low socio-economic status school communities*. Canberra, Australian Government Printing Service.

Cranston, N., Mulford, B., Keating, J. and Reid, A. (2010). Primary school principals and the purposes of schooling in Australia. *Journal of Educational Administration*, 48 (4), 517–539.

Darling-Hammond, L. and Wood, G. (eds) (2008). *Democracy at risk: The need for a new federal policy in education*. Washington, DC, Forum for Education and Democracy.

De Waal, A. (2006). Do targets work? *Times Education Supplement*, 19 August.

Department for Education (DfE) (2010). *The importance of teaching: Schools White Paper*. London, DfE.

Department for Education (DfE) (2013). What is an academy? From www.education.gov.uk/schools/leadership/typesofschools/academies/b00205692/whatisanacademy, accessed 10 March 2015.

Dingerson, L., Peterson, B. and Miner, B. (2008). Introduction. In L. Dingerson, B. Peterson and B. Miner (eds) *Keeping the promise? The debate over charter schools*. Milwaukee, WI, Rethinking Schools Ltd.

Eacott, S. (2011). New look at leaders or a new look at leadership? *International Journal of Educational Management*, 25 (2), 134–143.

Education Queensland (2006). *Leadership matters: Leadership capabilities for Education Queensland principals*. Brisbane, Department of Education, Training and the Arts.

English, F. W. (2000). Psssssst! What does one call a set of non-empirical beliefs required to be accepted on faith and enforced by authority? (Answer: a religion, aka the ISLLC standards). *International Journal of Leadership in Education*, 3 (2), 159–167.

English, F. W. (2003). Cookie-cutter leaders for cookie-cutter schools: The teleology of standardization and the de-legitimization of the university in educational leadership preparation. *Leadership and Policy in Schools*, 2 (1), 27–46.

English, F. W. (2006). The unintended consequences of a standardized knowledge base in advancing educational leadership preparation. *Educational Administration Quarterly*, 42 (3), 461–472.

Evans, L. (2011). The 'shape' of teacher professionalism in England: Professional standards, performance management, professional development and the changes proposed in the 2010 White Paper. *British Educational Research Journal*, 37 (5), 851–870.

Exley, S. and Ball. S. (2011). Something old, something new . . . understanding Conservative education policy. In H. Bochel (ed.) *The Conservative Party and social policy*. Bristol, Policy Press.

Fabricant, M. and Fine, M. (2012). *Charter schools and the corporate makeover of public education*. New York, Teachers College Press.

Fullan, M. (2002). The change leader. *Educational Leadership*, 59 (8), 16–21.

Gale, T. and Densmore, K. (2000). *Just schooling*. Buckingham, Open University Press.

Gerwitz, S., Ball, S. J. and Bowe, R. (1995). *Markets, choice and equity in education*. Buckingham, Open University Press.

Gillies, D. (2008). Developing governmentality: Conduct and education policy. *Journal of Education Policy*, 23 (4), 415–427.

Gillies, D. (2013). *Educational leadership and Michel Foucault*. New York, Routledge.

Giroux, H. A. (2003). Public pedagogy and the politics of resistance: Notes on a critical theory of educational struggle. *Educational Philosophy and Theory*, 35 (1), 5–16.

Glatter, R. (2012). Persistent preoccupations: The rise and rise of school autonomy and accountability in England. *Educational Management Administration and Leadership*, 40 (5), 559–575.

Gorard, S. (2005). Current contexts for research in educational leadership and management. *Educational Management Administration and Leadership*, 33 (2), 155–164.

Gorard, S. (2009). What are academies the answer to? *Journal of Education Policy*, 24 (1), 101–113.

Grimaldi, E. (2012). Neoliberalism and the marginalisation of social justice: The making of an educational policy to combat social exclusion. *International Journal of Inclusive Education*, 16 (11), 1131–1154.

Gunter, H. (2012). *Leadership and the reform of education*. Bristol, Policy Press.

Gunter, H. (ed.) (2013). *Educational leadership and Hannah Arendt*. London, Routledge.

Gunter, H., Thomson, P. and Blackmore, J. (2013). Series foreword. In H. Gunter (ed.) *Educational leadership and Hannah Arendt*. London, Routledge.

Hadfield, M. (2005). From networking to school networks to 'networked' learning: The challenge for the Network Learning Communities programme. In W. Veuglelers and M. J. O'Hair (eds) *Network learning for educational change*. Maidenhead, Open University Press/McGraw-Hill Education.

Hardy, I. and Boyle, C. (2011). My school? Critiquing the abstraction and quantification of education. *Asia Pacific Journal of Teacher Education*, 39 (3), 211–222.

Hargreaves, D. (2011). System redesign for system capacity building. *Journal of Educational Administration*, 49 (6), 685–700.

Hayes, D., Christie, P., Mills, M. and Lingard, R. (2004). Productive leaders and productive leadership. *Journal of Educational Administration*, 42 (5), 520–538.

Hayes, D., Mills, M., Christie, P. and Lingard, R. (2006). *Teachers and schooling: Making a difference*. Crows Nest, Allen and Unwin.

Heslop, J. (2003). Living and teaching in Aboriginal communities. In Q. Beresford and G. Partington (eds) *Reform and Resistance in Aboriginal Education*. Crawley, University of Western Australia Press.

Hill, R. (2010). *Chain reactions: A thinkpiece on the development of chains of schools in the English school system*. Nottingham, National College for School Leadership.

Hill, R., Dunford, J., Parish, N., Rea, S. and Sandals, R. (2012). *The growth of academy chains: Implications for leaders and leadership*. Nottingham, National College for School Leadership.

Jorgensen, R., Grootenboer, P., Niesche, R. and Lerman, S. (2010). Challenges for teacher education: The mis-match between beliefs and practice in remote Indigenous contexts. *Asia Pacific Journal of Teacher Education*, 38 (2), 161–175.

Jorgensen, R. and Niesche, R. (2011). Curriculum leadership in remote Indigenous communities. *Leading and Managing*, 17 (1), 45–58.

Keddie, A. (2012). *Educating for diversity and social justice*. New York, Routledge.

Keddie, A. (2014). 'It's like Spiderman . . . with great power comes great responsibility': School autonomy and the audit culture. *School Leadership and Management*, 34 (5), 502–517.

Keddie, A. and Mills, M. (2007). *Teaching boys: Classroom practices that work*. Crows Nest, Allen and Unwin.

Keddie, A. and Niesche, R. (2012). Productive engagements with student difference: Supporting equity through cultural recognition. *British Educational Research Journal*, 38 (2), 333–348.

Kellerman, B. (2012). *The end of leadership*. New York, HarperCollins.

Knight, J. (1994). Social justice and effective schooling. *Education Views*, 3 (8), 8.

Ladson-Billings, G. (1995). Toward a theory of culturally relevant pedagogy. *American Educational Research Journal*, 32 (3), 465–491.

Ladson-Billings, G. and Gillborn, D. (eds) (2004). *The RoutledgeFalmer reader in multicultural education*. London, RoutledgeFalmer.

Lakomski, G. (2005). *Managing without leadership: Towards a theory of organizational functioning*. London, Elsevier.

Lamb, S. (2007). School reform and inequality in urban Australia: A case study of residualising the poor. In R. Teese, S. Lamb and M. Duru-Bellat M (eds) *International studies in inequality, theory and policy*, Volume 3: *Education theory and public policy*. Dordrecht, Springer.

Lawson, H., Boyask, R. and Waite, S. (2013). Construction of difference and diversity within policy and practice in England. *Cambridge Journal of Education*, 43 (1), 107–122.

Leys, C. (2003). *Market-driven politics: Neoliberal democracy and the public interest*. New York, Verso.

Lingard, R. (2010). Policy borrowing, policy learning: Testing times in Australian schooling. *Critical Studies in Education*, 51 (2), 129–147.

Lingard, R. (2011). Policy as numbers: Ac/counting for educational research. *Australian Educational Researcher*, 38 (4), 355–382.

Lingard, R., Hayes, D. and Mills, M. (2002). Developments in school based management. *Journal of Educational Administration*, 40 (1), 6–30.

Lingard, R., Hayes, D., Mills, M. and Christie, P. (2003). *Leading learning*. Maidenhead, Open University Press.

Lingard, R. and Sellar, S. (2012). A policy sociology reflection on school reform in England: From the 'Third Way' to the 'Big Society'. *Journal of Educational Administration and History*, 44 (1), 43–63.

Lingard, R. et al. (2001). *The Queensland school reform longitudinal study*. Brisbane, Education Queensland.

Lipman, P. (2011). *The new political economy of urban education: Neoliberalism, race and the right to the city*. New York, Routledge.

Lupton, R. (2011). 'No change there then!' The onward march of school markets and competition. *Journal of Educational Administration and History*, 43 (4), 309–323.

Lyotard, J. F. (1984). *The postmodern condition: A report on knowledge*. Translated by G. Bennington and B. Massumi. Minneapolis, University of Minnesota Press.

Marshall, C. (2004). Social justice challenges to educational administration: Introduction to a special issue. *Educational Administration Quarterly*, 40 (3), 3–13.

Masters, G. (2009). *A shared challenge: Improving literacy, numeracy and science learning in Queensland primary schools*. Melbourne, ACER.

Matthews, P. and Berwick, G. (2013). *Teaching schools: First among equals?* Nottingham, National College for Teaching and Leadership.

McConaghy, C. (2000). *Rethinking Indigenous education: Culturalism, colonialism, and the politics of knowing*. Flaxton, Post Pressed.

McNamara, O. (2013). The School Direct programme and its implications for research informed teacher education and teacher educators. In L. Florian and N. Pantic (eds) *Learning to teach*. York, Higher Education Academy.

Melbourne University (2013). *Evaluation of the Independent Public Schools initiative*. Melbourne, University of Melbourne, on behalf of Department of Education, WA. From www.education.wa.edu.au/home/detcms/navigation/about-us/programs-and-initiatives/independent-public-schools/?page=6, accessed 18 March 2015.

Mills, C. and Gale, T. (2010). *Schooling in disadvantaged communities*. New York, Springer.

Morrison, M., Lumby, J. and Sood, K. (2006). Diversity and diversity management: Messages from recent research. *Educational Management Administration and Leadership*, 34 (3), 277–295.

Muijs, D. (2011). Leadership and organisational performance: From research to prescription? *International Journal of Educational Management*, 25 (1), 45–60.

Muijs, D., Ainscow, M., Chapman, C. and West, M. (2011). *Collaboration and networking in education*. London, Springer.

Munns, G. (2007). A sense of wonder: Pedagogies to engage students who live in poverty. *International Journal of Inclusive Education*, 11 (3), 301–315.

Myhill, D. (2006). Talk, talk, talk: Teaching and learning in whole class discourse. *Research Papers in Education*, 21 (1), 19–41.

National College for School Leadership (2011). *National Teaching Schools prospectus*. Nottingham, National College for Teaching and Leadership.

National College for Teaching and Leadership. (2014). *Teaching schools: A guide for potential applicants*. From www.gov.uk/teaching-schools-a-guide-for-potential-applicants, accessed 10 March 2015.

Newmann, F. M. and associates. (1996). *Authentic achievement: Restructuring schools of intellectual quality*. San Francisco, CA, Jossey Bass.

Newmann, F. M., Secada, W. and Wehlage, G. (1995). *A guide to authentic instruction and assessment: Vision, standards and scoring*. Madison, WI, Wisconsin Center for Education Research.

Niesche, R. (2012). Politicising articulation: Applying Lyotard's work to the use of standards in educational leadership. *International Journal of Leadership in Education*, 16 (2), 220–233.

Niesche, R. (2013). *Deconstructing educational leadership: Derrida and Lyotard*. London, Routledge.

Niesche, R. and Keddie, A. (2011). Foregrounding issues of equity and diversity in educational leadership. *School Leadership and Management*, 31 (1), 65–77.

Normore, A. H. (ed.) (2008). *Educational leadership for social justice*. North Carolina, Information Age.

Office for Standards in Education (Ofsted) (2010). *The London challenge*. From www.ofsted.gov.uk/resources/london-challenge, accessed 10 March 2015.

Organisation for Economic Cooperation and Development (OECD) (2007). *Education at a glance*. From www.oecd.org/education/skills-beyond-school/39313286.pdf, accessed 10 March 2015.

Organisation for Economic Cooperation and Development (OECD) (2011). *School autonomy and accountability: Are they related to school performance?* From www.oecd.org/pisa/pisaproducts/pisainfocus/ 48910490.pdf, accessed 10 March 2015.

Organisation for Economic Cooperation and Development (OECD) (2014). *Education at a Glance 2014.* From www.oecd.org/edu/ Education-at-a-Glance-2014.pdf, accessed 18 March 2015.

Osborne, D. and Gaebler, T. (1992). *Reinventing government: How the entrepreneurial spirit is transforming the public sector.* New York, Penguin.

Ozga, J. (2009). Governing education though data in England: From regulation to self-evaluation. *Journal of Education Policy*, 24 (2), 149–162.

Pennell, H. and West, A. (2009). Campaigns by parents to set up new schools in England: Issues and barriers. *Educational Studies*, 35 (1), 37–52.

Power, M. (1997). *The audit society: Rituals of verification.* Oxford, Oxford University Press.

Ravitch, D. (2010). *The death and life of the American school system: How testing and choice are undermining education.* Philadelphia, PA, Basic.

Rizvi, F. and Lingard, R. (2010). *Globalizing education policy.* London, Routledge.

Rose, N. (1999). *Powers of freedom: Reframing political thought.* Cambridge, Cambridge University Press.

Rothstein, R. (2004). *Class and schools: Using social, economic and educational reform to close the black–white achievement gap.* New York, Teachers College Press.

Russell, M. (2005). Untapped talent and unlimited potential: African American students and the science pipeline. *Negro Educational Review*, 56 (2–3), 167–182.

Ryan, J. (1998). Critical leadership for education in a postmodern world: Emancipation, resistance and communal action. *International Journal of Leadership in Education*, 1 (3), 257–278.

Ryan, J. (2010). Promoting social justice in schools: Principals' political strategies. *International Journal of Leadership in Education*, 13 (4), 357–376.

Sahlberg, P. (2011). *Finnish lessons: What can the world learn from educational change in Finland.* New York, Teachers College Press.

Sammons, P., Mujtaba, T., Earl, L. and Gu, Q. (2007). Participation in network learning community programmes and standards of pupil achievement: Does it make a difference? *School Leadership and Management*, 27 (3), 213–238.

Sarra, C. (2003). *Cherbourg State School, strong and smart, What Works program: Improving outcomes for Indigenous students*. From http://www.whatworks.edu.au/dbAction.do?cmd=displaySitePage1andsubcmd=selectandid=111, accessed 10 March 2015.

Shields, C. M. (2003). *Good intentions are not enough: Transformative leadership for communities of difference*. Lanham, MD, Scarecrow.

Shields, C. M. (2004). Dialogic leadership for social justice: Overcoming pathologies of silence. *Educational Administration Quarterly*, 40 (1), 109–132.

Shields, C. M. (2010). Transformative leadership: Working for equity in diverse contexts. *Educational Administration Quarterly*, 46 (4), 558–589.

Sliwka, A. (2003). Networking for educational innovation: A comparative analysis. In D. Istance and M. Kobayashi (eds) *Schooling for tomorrow: Networks of innovation – towards new models for managing schools and school systems*. Paris, OECD.

Smyth, J. (2011). The disaster of the 'self managing school': Genesis, trajectory, undisclosed agenda, and effects. *Journal of Educational Administration and History*, 43 (2), 95–117.

Steering Committee for the Review of Government Service Provision (2007). *Overcoming Indigenous disadvantage: Key indicators 2007*. Canberra, Commonwealth Government.

Suspitsyna, T. (2010). Accountability in American education as a rhetoric and a technology of governmentality. *Journal of Educational Policy*, 25 (5), 567–586.

Teese, R. and Polesel, J. (2003). *Undemocratic schooling: Equity and quality in mass secondary education in Australia*. Melbourne, Melbourne University Press.

Theoharis, G. (2007). Social justice educational leaders and resistance: Toward a theory of social justice. *Educational Administration Quarterly*, 43 (2), 221–258.

Theoharis, G. (2010). Disrupting injustice: Principals narrate the strategies they use to improve their schools and advance social justice. *Teachers College Record*, 112 (1), 331–373.

Thomson, P. (2009). *Heads on the block*. London and New York, Routledge.

Thrupp, M. (2003). The school leadership literature in managerialist times: Exploring the problem of textual apologism. *School Leadership and Management*, 23 (2), 149–172.

Thrupp, M. and Willmott, R. (2003). *Educational management in managerialist times*. Maidenhead, Open University Press.

Watterston, J. and Caldwell, B. (2011). System alignment as a key strategy in building capacity for school transformation. *Journal of Educational Administration*, 49 (6), 637–652.

West, A. (2010). High stakes testing, accountability, incentives and consequences in English schools. *Policy and Politics*, 38 (1), 23–39.

West, A. and Bailey, E. (2013). The development of the academies programme: 'Privatising' school-based education in England 1986–2013, *British Journal of Educational Studies*, 61 (2), 137–159.

West, A. and Pennell, H. (2000). Publishing school examination results in England: Incentives and consequences. *Educational Studies*, 26 (4), 423–436.

West, A. and Ylönen, A. (2010). Market-oriented school reform in England and Finland: School choice, finance and governance. *Educational Studies*, 36 (1), 1–12.

Wilkins, A. (2012). Public battles and private takeovers: Academies and the politics of educational governance. *Journal of Pedagogy*, 3 (1), 11–29.

Wilkinson, J. (2008). Good intentions are not enough: A critical examination of diversity and educational leadership scholarship. *Journal of Educational Administration and History*, 40 (2), 101–112.

Wilkinson, R. and Pickett, K. (2009). *The spirit level: Why greater equality makes societies stronger*. New York, Bloomsbury Press.

Williamson, J. and Dalal, P. (2007). Indigenising the curriculum or negotiating the tensions at the cultural interface? Embedding Indigenous perspectives and pedagogies in a university curriculum. *Australian Journal of Indigenous Education*, 36 (Supplementary), 51–58.

Wright, N. (2001). Leadership, 'bastard leadership' and managerialism: Confronting twin paradoxes in the Blair education project. *Educational Management and Administration*, 29 (3), 275–290.

Wright, N. (2011). Between 'bastard' and 'wicked' leadership? School leadership and the emerging policies of the UK coalition government. *Journal of Educational Administration and History*, 43 (4), 345–362.

Wu, M. (2010). Measurement, sampling and equating errors on large-scale assessments. *Educational Measurement: Issues and Practice*, 29 (4), 15–27.

3   Theoretical tools

In this chapter we introduce the theoretical tools and concepts on which we draw in this book to think about, analyse and explain the two case studies. Broadly speaking, we draw on Foucault's notions of power, subjectivity and ethics to understand the work of leaders and schools in pursuing an agenda of social justice and equity. In the first part of the chapter we introduce Foucault's work on power, resistance and the subject. We then shift to examining his later work on ethics, specifically his fourfold frame of *ethical substance, modes of subjection, forms of elaboration* and *telos*. Foucault's work on ethics is intrinsic to notions of technologies and practices of the self. We explain how this notion of ethics was developed out of his earlier work on discourse, knowledge and genealogies of power to provide an analysis of the subject that allows for action that we examine in the case studies.

After briefly introducing Foucault's fourfold ethical framework, we articulate the theoretical utility of the concept of telos, in terms of assisting us to theorise the ethical approach to leadership and social justice reflected in the case study data, and modes of subjection as the parameters of official education policy that shape the work of educational leaders in working towards their particular telos. The chapter then turns to an explanation of three key theoretical tools: truth-telling, advocacy and counter-conduct. Within the context of Foucault's fourfold ethical framework we conceptualise and present these tools as forms of ethical elaboration. Such tools are significant to the ethical approach to leadership and social justice taken up by Carol as principal of Ridgeway and the leaders of the Clementine-led alliance. These tools support these leaders to work towards their telos of leadership and social justice within the context of specific moral codes or modes of subjection.

As noted in Chapter 1, we present these ethical tools as requisite to pursuing socially just leadership within the demands of the current climate. We will illustrate in this chapter how they help leaders to address

the multidimensionality of injustices confronting schools and education systems – their economic, cultural and political dimensions (see
Fraser, 2009).

We acknowledge the broad expanse and complexity of the work that
Foucault has contributed to the world of theory and philosophy within
numerous domains and areas. We present here a specific representation
of his work. This presentation is not intended to minimise the significance, breadth and complexity of his work. Our explication of Foucault's
theories in what follows is intended to illuminate the utility of specific
tools not only in making sense of our case study data in relation to the
specific focus of this book – leadership, ethics and schooling for social
justice – but also in generating new insights and ways of thinking about
this focus.

Michel Foucault

Michel Foucault was a powerfully influential French thinker whose
work continues to be used extensively throughout the humanities
and social sciences today. The application of his ideas in education is
incredibly vast, so much so that we cannot possibly do justice to all of
this work here. Some useful examples for those new to Foucault's work
in education include Ball (1990, 2013), McNicol Jardine (2005), Peters
and Besley (2007) and Usher and Edwards (1994), to name a few. More
specifically for our purposes in this book, Foucault's ideas have been used
extensively in critical management and organisation studies (see Barley
and Kunda, 1992; McKinlay and Starkey, 1998; Miller and O'Leary,
1989; Townley, 1993; Fleming and Spicer, 2007), and have also enjoyed
increasing popularity in educational leadership and management studies
(Anderson and Grinberg, 1998; Ball, 1994; Gillies, 2013; Hultqvist and
Dahlberg, 2001; Niesche, 2011; Popkewitz and Brennan, 1997, 1998).
These important contributions, among others, have introduced Foucault's
work, particularly on power, resistance and the subject, into educational
leadership and management, which as a 'field' has traditionally avoided
engaging with these sorts of more 'critical' approaches. Foucault's work
is difficult for educational leadership scholars and writers not only
because he said little about education (and nothing about educational
leadership), but also because his ideas challenge and problematise the
foundations of the modernist education project and the instrumentalism
of leadership studies.

Gillies (2013) and Niesche (2011) both suggest that Foucault's ideas
can be used to trouble educational leadership discourse and argue that
they provide the tools to think differently and more generatively about
the field of educational leadership, management and administration.

We believe this latter point is important, and it is the focus of how we use Foucault's work in this book. It would be easy, as many others have done, simply to use Foucault's work to outline how education and leadership can operate as forms of discipline and control. However, our purpose here is to draw specifically upon Foucault's later work on ethics and the subject to show how his work can illuminate particular leadership practices in working towards a particular goal, mode of being or telos.

Power, resistance and the subject

Foucault is well known for developing a detailed analysis of the emergence and operations of modern forms of power across a number of specific fields. Through the analysis of power and regimes of practices in the areas of insanity and mental illness (Foucault, 1967), hospitals and medicine (Foucault, 1975), prisons (Foucault, 1977) and sexuality (Foucault, 1981), Foucault develops some key themes for understanding the production of knowledge and subjects in modern societies. In contrast to more traditional and sovereign notions of power, Foucault conceptualises power not as something that is possessed, or that exists as a form of repression or domination. According to Foucault, power is a relation *between* individuals or groups of individuals, not a thing that is held or owned by individuals to be used. Power is something that is exercised, or is 'a set of actions upon other actions' (Foucault, 2002b: 341). Power is exercised through networks of relations rather than individuals simply being at the point of its application (Foucault, 1980).

Foucault was also very clear that he was not developing a theory of power but rather tools for analysis of the subject. As he states, 'while the human subject is placed in relations of production and of signification, he is equally placed in power relations that are very complex' (Foucault, 2002b: 327). Foucault's work analyses the forms of power that are applied in everyday life:

> This form of power that applies itself to immediate everyday life categorizes the individual, marks him [*sic*][1] by his own individuality, attaches him to his own identity, imposes a law of truth on him that he must recognize and have others recognize in him. It is a form of power that makes individuals subjects.
>
> (Foucault, 2002b: 331)

Foucault uses the term 'subject' to refer to two things: first, subject to someone else's control and dependence; and, second, tied to one's own identity by a conscience or self-knowledge (Foucault, 2002b: 331).

According to Foucault, the subject is constituted and shaped by and through various discourses that are intimately linked to social structures and practices. The subject is placed in complex sets of power relations, and it is these relations that should be analysed. The school principal, for instance, is constituted through intersecting discourses as they subject others (for example, teachers and students) through their pronouncements and actions; and they are also the target of, and subjected to, particular leadership, managerialist and disciplinary practices and discourses themselves (see Niesche, 2011).

Foucault's notion of resistance was first developed in Volume I of *The History of Sexuality*, where he claims that 'where there is power, there is resistance' and 'consequently this resistance is never in a position of exteriority to power' (Foucault, 1981: 95). It is in the relational character of power relationships that Foucault highlights a multiplicity or plurality of points of resistance: that is, they are present everywhere in the networks of power. The importance of Foucault's conceptualisation of resistance lies in the idea that resistance operates as a part of power, not in opposition to it or against it. For instance, Scott (1985, 1990) shows how resistance can be formulated in numerous ways and argues that one needs to be aware of the hidden transcripts of resistance. As Scott (1990: 20) argues, 'neither everyday forms of resistance nor the occasional insurrection can be understood without references to the sequestered social sites of which resistance can be nurtured and given meaning'. These sequestered social sites need to be acknowledged and explored in the ways that school principals exercise forms of everyday resistance to top-down compliance procedures.

Foucault would later provide some further thinking on this notion of power, resistance and the limits of power. The following is an excerpt from two lectures he gave in 1979, in which he articulated a more 'usable' notion of power:

> A man who is chained up and beaten is subject to force being exerted over him, not power. But if he can be induced to speak, when his ultimate recourse could have been to hold his tongue, preferring death, then he has been subjected to power. He has been submitted to government. If an individual can remain free, however little his freedom may be, power can subject him to government. There is no power without refusal or revolt . . . Consequently those who resist or reel against a form of power cannot merely be content to denounce violence or criticize an institution. Nor is it enough to cast blame on reason in general. What has to be questioned is the form of rationality at stake.
>
> (Foucault, 2002a: 324)

While used only sparsely throughout this book, these specific notions of power, resistance and the subject are key to providing the context for Foucault's later work on ethics. This quote was one of Foucault's earliest accounts of his notion of resistance. This understanding of resistance was underdeveloped, and it wasn't until the later publication of his extensive lecture series that his further work in this area came to light. These points are significant as they serve to illustrate the precursor to his later theorising of counter-conduct, rather than using the term 'resistance'.

There have been debates among scholars as to the nature of the shifts in Foucault's theorising throughout his work and life, and whether his work on ethics should be seen as a continuation of his previous projects or a radical departure. However, it is important to have some knowledge of how these ideas have evolved and in fact continue to play a part in his writing on ethics and can add some understanding to how Foucault conceptualises technologies of the self and the constitution of the subject through particular practices. We articulate these ideas in the next section.

Foucault's ethics

As we have already stated, the notion of the subject is central to Foucault's work (Foucault, 2002b). While the term 'subject' has been used in various ways, Foucault generally uses it to refer to an entity that is able to choose courses of action in the sense of being controlled by others and also in the sense of being attached to an identity through awareness and knowledge of self (O'Farrell, 2005: 110). Through Foucault's genealogical project examining the history of the formation of the subject – that is, the ways in which individuals are transformed into subjects – he emphasises the notion that the subject is not fixed or existing prior to history and truth. Rather, the subject is dissolved and recreated in different ways through various knowledges and practices (Foucault, 2002b). Therefore, there is no true self that is waiting to be discovered. The self is in fact constituted as the subject of his/her own actions through the relationship with his/her history, society and culture (Foucault, 2000). Subjects are not only shaped by social structures but actively take up their own discourses through which they are shaped and by which they shape themselves. Davies's (2004: 7; emphasis in original) understanding of subjects is also useful here:

> People exist at the points of intersection of multiple discursive practices, those points being conceptualized as subject positions. *The individual is not fixed at any one of these points or locations.* Not only does the individual shift locations or positions, but what each location or position might mean shifts over space and time and contexts.

Throughout the case studies presented later in this book we take the view that the subject is a site of disunity, tension and struggle (Ball and Olmedo, 2013; Weedon, 1987). These competing subject positions are informed by a range of discourses.

In Foucault's later work his concern was with ethics and the relationship one has with oneself. This work should also be understood as being situated at the intersection of his themes of a history of subjectivity and his analysis of forms of governmentality (Davidson, 2005). This means that there is a clear link between the relationship of the self to itself but also in the governing of others. For example, Foucault (2000: 300) states:

> Governmentality implies the relationship of the self to the self, and I intend this concept of governmentality to cover the whole range of practices that constitute, define, organize and instrumentalize the strategies that individuals in their freedom can use in dealing with each other. Those who try to control, determine and limit the freedom of others are themselves free individuals who have at their disposal certain instruments they can use to govern others.

This bringing out of the freedom of the subject and its relationship to others is an important aspect of governmentality and also of ethical work. Foucault refers to ethics as 'the considered form that freedom takes when it is informed by reflection' (Foucault, 2000: 284). This is in contrast to the term 'morals', by which Foucault means the sets of values and rules of action that are often prescribed by institutions such as churches, families, schools and so on. Foucault believes that it is the relationship that one has with these prescribed codes of action that is important: that is, how one conducts oneself in relation to these moral codes. Ethics is not the field of rules or principles but the formation of one's self-constitution as a subject (O'Leary, 2002: 11). Elaborating on this, Foucault uses a fourfold ethical framework to designate those aspects of ethical work consisting of various technologies of the self and in the governing of others. Foucault (1990, 1992) refers to these four aspects as:

- *Ethical substance*, or the part of oneself or one's behaviour that is to be considered for ethical judgement for the purposes of moral conduct. According to Foucault, for the ancient Greeks, this consisted of acts linked with pleasure and desire. It could also refer to aspects such as emotions and sexuality, for example. In this book we explore the leadership of principals as a form of ethical substance in the case studies as they undertake their work in their schools.

- *Modes of subjection*, or the ways in which individuals are made to think about or recognise their moral obligations. This can take the form of holy texts such as the Bible or the Qur'an and also laws and social customs. The local communities, students, parents and education authorities themselves form powerful modes of subjection for the principals of the schools we discuss in this book in relation to their ethical and moral articulations about what might constitute good leadership and practice within their schools.
- *Forms of elaboration*, or the self-forming activities or practices through which individuals constitute themselves as ethical subjects. These could consist of particular leadership practices that are necessary to transform oneself into an ethical subject or particular practices seen as necessary to alleviate poverty or disadvantage.
- *Telos*, or a particular mode of being that is characteristic of an ethical subject. This could be the kind of principal or leader one aims to be, and the focus/purpose of this leadership. In this book we articulate a telos of leadership and social justice as put forward by the principals and their school communities.

This fourfold framework is useful not for the purposes of characterising or capturing a linear identity formation or prescribed form of best leadership practice, but rather to examine how individuals constitute themselves as ethical subjects. This can be a particularly useful notion when considering the work of school leaders as they are implicitly working ethically on themselves and in the governing of their schools, communities and (in the case of the England case study) other schools. As we particularly draw on the aspects of telos, modes of subjection and forms of elaboration in the later chapters, we will now examine these in more depth.

Telos

As stated above, telos refers to the teleology of the moral subject – a particular mode of being or goal towards which one aims in the ethical work carried out on the self (O'Leary, 2002). More specifically for Foucault, the process of ethical self-formation is one:

> In which the individual delimits that part of himself that will form the object of his moral practice, defines his position relative to the precept he will follow, and decides on a certain mode of being that will serve as his moral goal. And this requires him to act upon himself, to monitor, test, improve, and transform himself.
>
> (Foucault, 1992: 28)

According to Foucault (1992: 28), these actions conform not only to other actions in relation to rules and values, but also to a certain mode of being, an aspirational form of mastery of the self, or 'a perfect tranquility of soul, a total insensitivity to the agitations of the passions, or toward a purification that will ensure salvation after death and blissful immortality'. Here, Foucault is concerned with 'an aesthetics of existence' to articulate the kind of self one's self-transformation will take in working towards an ideal. It was Foucault's desire to see the formation of the subject as a form of expressed freedom in relation to punitive codes (O'Leary, 2002), or, in the case of the principals and school leaders in our case studies, punitive forms of accountability and surveillance that prescribe a limited range of subject positionings in which to work towards mandated education reforms and goals.

We have used telos in the case study analyses in two key ways. First, in relation to leadership relations: for example, in Chapters 4 and 5, the relations Carol has with her teachers, including the different types of leadership on which she draws and the significance of context in how she draws on these types of leadership; and for the Clementine-led alliance in Chapters 6 and 7, the leadership relations deployed by Clementine to foster collaboration with other schools. And, second, in relation to social justice: for example, the challenges associated in both case study school contexts with supporting all students to achieve academic and schooling success. These teloi are governed or regulated within particular parameters as modes of subjection.

Modes of subjection

For Foucault (1992: 27), the mode of subjection is 'the way in which the individual establishes his relation to the rule and recognizes himself as obliged to put it into practice'. In other words, a mode of subjection is the way in which one brings oneself to follow, or not follow, a code, and/or because one recognises oneself as a member of a particular community (O'Leary, 2002). There is an aspect to the modes of subjection that is a questioning of why one should be engaged in a particular practice. What are the elements, discourses or vehicles by which one is expected or required to act? For instance, in education there are whole discourses, policies and documents that one must consider as modes of subjection to the work that one does on the self in order to become a good principal or teacher. For teachers, powerful modes of subjection come in the form of teacher standards and accreditation, but also teachers' professional associations and parental, student and societal expectations. These are the factors that allow a teacher to recognise their obligations in the work they must do to become the kind of teacher they wish to be, to work towards a particular telos. There are similar sorts of expectations for school leaders and principals in the work they must do.

There is not only a recognition that one must work on the self with these modes of subjection in mind, but also that these can be resisted if there is a tension between expectations and the way one must work in relation to these expectations to achieve a teleology of the subject. Foucault (2002b: 216) states, 'maybe the task nowadays is one of rejecting the forms of subjectivity and the modes of subjectivation which are imposed on us'. Here, he is suggesting that in order to work towards an ideal self (the telos), it may be necessary to resist or exercise forms of counter-conduct against and within the spaces of powerful modes of subjection. One of the central themes we move to next is this idea of counter-conduct and truth-telling as key aspects of formation of the self. In fact, we make the case that it is necessary to undertake these practices if one is to work against powerful neoliberal discourses of education to further issues of social justice and equity. These modes of subjection are not all powerful: they can be resisted and challenged, as the two case studies illustrate. Foucault's emphasis on the hermeneutics of the self in his later works illustrates his desire to show that individuals are not helplessly subject (O'Leary, 2002) to the repressive, punitive mechanisms of certain moral codes. It is this refusal of an imposed self that Foucault's ethics addresses as a central concern.

We now turn to look at these means of resistance, forms of elaboration, that we employ as lenses through which to analyse the practices of the leaders in the two case study schools.

Forms of elaboration: truth-telling, advocacy and counter-conduct

We interpret the notions of truth-telling, advocacy and counter-conduct as working within Foucault's framework as forms of elaboration: that is, they are the practices through which the leaders in this book constitute themselves as ethical subjects whose efforts to pursue social justice involve advocating for others and speaking out against, or engaging in, conduct to counter the injustices of the status quo. Below, we elaborate on these concepts and their utility as analytical tools for understanding the case study data.

Parrhesia or 'truth-telling'

In the book *Fearless Speech* (2001), as well as in the more recently translated lecture series (Foucault, 2011, 2013), Foucault gives an evolution of the meaning of the term *parrhesia* through both ancient

Greek and Roman culture. He explains the term as referring to 'free speech' or 'speaking the truth' but more importantly indicates a particular relationship between the speaker and what they say. Foucault identifies the following five characteristics that are linked to parrhesia or a *parrhesiastes* (one who uses parrhesia).

Frankness

In parrhesia, the speaker gives a 'complete and exact account of what he has in mind so that the audience is able to comprehend exactly what the speaker thinks' (Foucault, 2001: 12). According to Foucault, this indicates a particular relationship between speaker and what they say, a certain social situation in which this occurs, and that what the parrhesiastes says is dangerous to herself/himself as it involves some form of risk. In parrhesia, the speaker is both the speaker and the subject of his/her own opinion. The relationship with the truth is an important aspect of parrhesia.

Truth

Foucault (2001: 14) claims that the parrhesiastes 'says what he knows to be true': that is, the speaker says what they believe to be true. They are sincere and have no doubt about what they speak. As Foucault says (2001: 15): 'The parrhesiatic game presupposes that the parrhesiastes is someone who has the moral qualities that are required, first, to know the truth, and secondly to convey such truth to others.' This implies that the speaker must have some form of authority on which to speak but at the same time is 'speaking up' to others, which involves a form of risk for the speaker.

The concept of parrhesia has utility in both of the case studies in making sense of advocacy work. In relation to Carol, the principal of Ridgeway, for example, we draw attention to her excellent position for engaging in parrhesia – in order to speak up to the education authorities and government bodies about issues that are pertinent to her students' and community's needs. As principal, she has this authority and knowledge. However, she is also at risk, because her job is at stake if she goes too far in what she says and does as principal. For Foucault, though, parrhesia is less about verifying that what the speaker says is 'true' and more about establishing a particular relationship between the speaker and what they say (Foucault, 2011).

Danger

Foucault uses the example of a philosopher telling a sovereign that he is being tyrannical and unjust in his decisions. The risk for the philosopher is that the sovereign may exile or even kill him. Therefore, parrhesia involves a form of risk, albeit not necessarily a risk to one's life, as in the case of Carol. What is important for Foucault (2001: 17) is that the speaker chooses a relationship to herself/himself that is one as truth-teller, not living by being false to oneself.

Criticism

Parrhesia entails criticism, either towards oneself or towards another. Importantly, though, the other is always in a position of authority over the speaker, thus there is risk.

Duty

Foucault clarifies that a prisoner who is forced to speak under duress, such as through torture, is not a parrhesiastes. However, if the prisoner were to volunteer a confession to a crime, then that would be a form of parrhesia. Parrhesia is always related to freedom and duty (Foucault, 2001: 19).

In summary of the above points, the Greeks believed that a parrhesiastes has the moral qualities that are required to tell the truth and convey that truth to others. There is a form of courage attached to this form of truth-telling as there is an element of risk that the speaker is saying something that is dangerous because it is different from what the majority believes. Foucault argues that a teacher imparting knowledge is not a parrhesiastes, but a philosopher speaking out against a sovereign is an example of parrhesia, because the philosopher is telling the sovereign something intolerable or unpleasant about their reign and, as such, is running the risk of possibly severe repercussions. Parrhesia is also a form of criticism 'from below': for example, from a student to a teacher. There is an element of risking one's position in order to speak freely, so a slave cannot be a parrhesiastes because they are unable to participate in 'the game'.

The significance of this notion for Foucault and for us in this book is that parrhesia indicates an example of how, through truth-telling, the individual is constituted as subject in their relationships to the self and others (Foucault, 2011: 42). For Foucault, one cannot attend to oneself without a relationship with others. In the case of school principals, then, they must constitute themselves as subject through their relationships with themselves and others, including teachers, parents and students. It is through the act of parrhesia that a principal will come to know and constitute himself or herself as an ethical subject. There is a relationship between the obligation to speak the truth, the techniques of governmentality and the constitution of the relationship to the self, in which the principal is a central actor. Parrhesia is a political structure (Foucault, 2011).

Advocacy

We also use the term 'advocacy' as an example of a form of elaboration of leaders in the case study schools speaking out for their schools and communities. This term in these contexts does not come from Foucault's oeuvre but rather from Gary Anderson's (2009) notion of 'advocacy leadership'. However, we are conceptualising this idea as a form of elaboration, a form of political subjectivity, that, in the case studies, exemplifies a key part of the ethical self-formation of the individual. Anderson uses the term 'advocacy leadership' not as another form of adjectival leadership to be implemented in the pursuit of effectiveness or productivity, but rather as an aspect of leadership that is inherently focused on advocacy for one's students and community. For instance, Anderson (2009: 13) says: 'I use the term advocacy leadership because I believe that a more politicized notion of leadership is needed that acknowledges that schools are sites of struggle over material and cultural resources and ideological commitments.' This means openly taking up the challenges of advocating for the basic principles of a high-quality and equitable public education for all children and being prepared to takes risks in working towards these aims (Anderson, 2009: 14). There must be some recognition of working on multiple levels in order to work against forms of discrimination, marginalisation and exclusion of students and community groups. It is very much about openly bringing the political into the leadership arena rather than attempting to remove it, as is often proposed by more traditional and conservative leadership discourses. This is leadership that works to address inequities in our education systems.

We acknowledge the long history of important work that has examined the problems of advocacy on behalf of marginalised groups. For example, while advocacy is often well intentioned, it can be imperialist and paternalistic and can thus work to reinstate the very relations of domination and oppression it seeks to alleviate (see Ellsworth, 1989). However, our focus is more about drawing on Foucault's tools to help illuminate and understand the work that leaders are doing as part of their own subject formation as ethical and political subjects and their schools as ethical institutions. As we discuss in Chapters 4–7, advocacy, it seems, is part of the ethical work that they consider important and it demands a significant amount of time and resources. Therefore, while not unproblematic at times, this form of advocacy is central to the school leaders' forms of elaboration, or the work that is done in the process of becoming a political subject.

Counter-conduct

Many scholars have discussed and applied Foucault's notion of govern-mentality to a range of fields and disciplines, but until recent years they had to rely mainly on his popular paper 'Governmentality' (Foucault, 1991). However, the publication of the complete lecture series in which 'Governmentality' was delivered has allowed interested parties to grasp more fully the scope and depth of Foucault's research into the develop-ment of the modern state and forms governmentality (Foucault, 2007, 2008). The term 'governmentality' – formed by combining the terms 'government' and 'mentality' – is often used to designate the rationality of government. Furthermore, Foucault regards governmentality as the 'conduct of conduct', meaning governments act by implementing particu-lar rationalities and mechanisms by which individuals' conduct is influenced and dictated. One aspect of this that seems to be particularly useful is Foucault's development of his notion of counter-conduct. Moving away from the term 'resistance' (and discarding other terms, such as 'dissidence', 'revolt' and 'insubordination'), Foucault develops the term 'counter-conduct' to refer to 'the sense of struggle against pro-cesses implemented for conducting others' (Foucault, 2007: 200–201). He admits that he is not altogether happy with this term, but he considers it preferable to the alternatives, given that 'counter-conduct' suggests an active sense of the word 'conduct'.

It is important to remember that Foucault's work at this point highlighted the interplay between church and state in modern Western societies, and more specifically the relationship between the pastorate and government (Foucault, 2008). For instance, in the series *Security, Territory, Population* he focused on how the pastorate constituted sets of techniques and procedures that showed the workings of pastoral power. We will not attempt to cover all of this here. The important point to note is how this notion of pastoral power links to Foucault's notion of conduct: that is, the conduct not of things but of people. Foucault argues that pastoral power is a highly specific form of governing individuals that must equally consider specific forms of resistance that appear at the same time. Some of the examples he gives relate to specific forms of revolt, and resistance and desertion in the military; the development of secret societies, such as the Freemasons; and forms of medical dissent, such as refusing vaccination (Foucault, 2008: 198–200). In discussing these practices, Foucault comes to the conclusion that 'counter-conduct' is the most appropriate term to use for them; also, importantly, his focus is on the practices, not the individual. He does this in order to avoid elements of 'hero worship', which he considers to be of little use as a form of analysis. As Foucault (2008: 202) states:

> There is a process of sanctification or hero worship which does not seem to me of much use. On the other hand, by using the word counter-conduct, and so without having to give a sacred status to this or that person as a dissident, we can no doubt analyze the components in the way in which someone actually acts in the very general field of politics or in the very general field of power relations; it makes it possible to pick out the dimension or component of counter-conduct that may well be found in delinquents, mad people, and patients. So an analysis of this immense family of what could be called counter-conducts.

This notion of analysing the practices rather than the person could prove useful in the field of educational leadership, which has long been fascinated by hero paradigms of leadership (Blackmore, 1999; Gronn, 2003). Foucault claims that it is the practices or the ways in which someone acts that are important. This then allows for an analysis of power or counter-conducts, rather than the study of the actual person. As such, this book focuses on leader and leadership practices and perceptions of practice as the most relevant factors. This works against the models of leadership that stress particular traits or characteristics of 'good leadership' or 'what counts' in school effectiveness and improvement, and thus casts a different line of thinking about school leadership practice.

We use the notion of counter-conduct to analyse the ways in which the leaders of the two case studies work to counter the modes of subjection that work to aims that do not align with their ideas of what is important and necessary in their schools and communities. As we argued in the previous chapter, the current fascination with neoliberal forms of governance and accountability, and with competition and choice as some of the key drivers of educational reform, works to perpetuate disadvantage and inequality and subsequent deficit discourses of disadvantaged students and communities. We put forward the notion that practices of counter-conduct are necessary to disrupt these powerful discourses in order for the leaders of these schools to bring about the desired changes that accompany their particular telos of what it means to be a good leader or principal and what their vision for the school might be. In both cases, these goals are closely aligned with principles of social justice and equity rather than compliance with highly hierarchical and performative forms of accountability.

Conclusion

In this chapter we have presented the key theoretical tools and concepts that inform our analysis of the case studies in the subsequent chapters. In particular, we have explained the utility of Foucault's fourfold ethical framework and his notions of parrhesia (including advocacy) and counter-conduct as specific examples of the forms of elaboration that he uses as one of the four frames. Our explication of these tools and theories illuminates their utility in understanding the work of leaders and schools that are seeking to address issues of social justice.

While Foucault spoke out against prescribing solutions or normative ideologies, we believe his work is very much directed with some alignment to socially just practices (O'Farrell, 2005). His analysis of regimes of practices, the inner workings of power and the formation of knowledge and his later emphasis on subjectivity and technologies of the self provide useful frames in which to understand the particular ways in which school leaders work towards certain aims and outcomes for themselves and their schools. We do not prescribe how these leaders should work, or what the telos of their leadership and school should be, other than to align these practices with Foucault's ethical framework. This is for the purpose of analysing the work involved in achieving socially just schooling, and to identify the constraints, limitations and potential space for action for school leaders to achieve their aims. Foucault (2000: 298–299) also cautions against those who might abuse the exercise of power:

> I see nothing wrong in the practices of a person who, knowing more than others in a specific game of truth, tells those others what to do, teaches them, and transmits knowledge and techniques to them. The problem in such practices where power – which is not in itself a bad thing – must inevitably come into play is knowing how to avoid the kind of domination effects where a kid is subjected to the arbitrary and unnecessary authority of a teacher . . . I believe that this problem must be framed in terms of rules of law, rational techniques of government, and ethos, practices of the self and freedom.

There are powerful forms of normalisation at work for school leaders, so it is important that they adopt 'a continual questioning and adjusting of thought in relation to notions of human good and harm' (Christie, 2005: 40). Christie further states that this must entail how to work on the self and how to act in relation to others. In the next chapter we begin the analysis of these practices in which school leaders are engaged, both on the self and in relation to others in their schools. The case of Carol and Ridgeway State High School is an example of one principal's continual questioning of and adjusting to the needs of that particular school community and often coming into tension with powerful modes of subjection from the education authorities.

Note

1 We acknowledge Foucault's preference for masculine pronouns as problematic, but we use '[*sic*]' only here, on the first appearance in this book, to avoid its repeated appearance throughout quotes from his work.

References

Anderson, G. (2009). *Advocacy leadership: Toward a post-reform agenda in education*. London and New York, Routledge.

Anderson, G. and Grinberg, J. (1998). Educational administration as a disciplinary practice: Appropriating Foucault's view of power, discourse, and method. *Educational Administration Quarterly*, 34 (3), 329–353.

Ball, S. J. (ed.) (1990). *Foucault and education: Disciplines and knowledge*. London and New York, Routledge.

Ball, S. J. (1994). Education reform: A critical and poststructural approach. Buckingham, Open University Press.

Ball, S. J. (2013). *Foucault, power and education*. New York and London, Routledge.

Ball, S. J. and Olmedo, A. (2013). Care of the self, resistance and subjectivity under neoliberal governmentalities. *Critical Studies in Education*, 54 (1), 85–96.

Barley, S. R. and Kunda, G. (1992). Design and devotion: Surges of rational and normative ideologies of control in managerial discourse. *Administrative Science Quarterly*, 37 (3), 363–399.

Blackmore, J. (1999). *Troubling women: Feminism, leadership and educational change*. Buckingham, Open University Press.

Christie, P. (2005). Education for an ethical imagination. *Social Alternatives*, 24 (4), 39–44.

Davidson, A. I. (2005). Ethics as aesthetics. In G. Gutting (ed.) *The Cambridge companion to Foucault*, 2nd edition. New York, Cambridge University Press.

Davies, B. (2004). Introduction: Poststructuralist lines of flight in Australia. *International Journal of Qualitative Studies in Education*, 17 (1), 3–9.

Ellsworth, E. (1989). Why doesn't this feel empowering? Working through the repressive myths of critical pedagogy. *Harvard Educational Review*, 59, 297–324.

Fleming, P. and Spicer, A. (2007). *Contesting the corporation: Struggle, power and resistance in organizations.* Cambridge, Cambridge University Press.

Foucault, M. (1967). *Madness and civilisation: A history of insanity in the age of reason.* London, Tavistock.

Foucault, M. (1975). *The birth of the clinic.* New York, Vintage.

Foucault, M. (1977). *Discipline and punish.* London, Penguin.

Foucault, M. (1980). Two lectures. In C. Gordon (ed.) *Power/knowledge: Selected interviews and other writings, 1972–1977.* Sussex, Harvester Press.

Foucault, M. (1981). *The history of sexuality,* Volume I. London, Penguin.

Foucault, M. (1990). *The history of sexuality,* Volume III: *The care of the self.* London, Penguin.

Foucault, M. (1991). Governmentality. In G. Burchill, C. Gordon and P. Miller (eds) *The Foucault effect: Studies in governmentality.* Chicago, University of Chicago Press.

Foucault, M. (1992). *The history of sexuality,* Volume II: *The use of pleasure.* Harmondsworth, Penguin.

Foucault, M. (2000). The ethics of the concern for self as a practice of freedom. In. P. Rabinow (ed.) *Essential works of Foucault 1954–1984,* Volume I: *Ethics.* London, Penguin.

Foucault, M. (2001). *Fearless speech.* Edited by J. Pearson. Los Angeles, CA, Semiotext(e).

Foucault, M. (2002a). Omnes et singulatem. In J. D. Faubion (ed.) *Essential works of Foucault, 1954–1984,* Volume I: *Power.* London, Penguin.

Foucault, M. (2002b). The subject and power. In J. D. Faubion (ed.) *Essential works of Foucault, 1954–1984,* Volume I: *Power.* London, Penguin.

Foucault, M. (2007). *Security, territory, population: Lectures at the College de France 1977–1978.* New York, Picador.

Foucault, M. (2008). *The birth of biopolitics: Lectures at the College de France 1978–1979.* New York, Picador.

Foucault, M. (2011). *The government of self and others: Lectures at the College de France 1982–1983.* Edited by F. Gros. Translated by G. Burchill. New York, Picador.

Foucault, M. (2013). *The courage of truth: Lectures at the College de France 1983–1984.* New York, Picador.

Fraser, N. (2009). *Scales of justice: Re-imagining political space in a globalizing world.* New York, Columbia University Press.

Gillies, D. (2013). *Educational leadership and Michel Foucault.* London and New York, Routledge.

Gronn, P. (2003). Leadership: Who needs it? *School Leadership and Management*, 23 (3), 267–290.

Hultqvist, K. and Dahlberg, G. (2001). *Governing the child in the new millennium*. London, Routledge.

McKinlay, A. and Starkey, K. (1998). Managing Foucault: Foucault, management and organisation theory. In A. McKinlay and K. Starkey (eds) *Foucault, management and organisation theory*. London, Sage.

McNicol Jardine, G. (2005). *Foucault and education*. New York, Peter Lang.

Miller, P. and O'Leary, T. (1989). Accounting and the construction of the governable person. *Accounting, organizations and society*, 12 (3), 235–265.

Niesche, R. (2011). *Foucault and educational leadership: Disciplining the principal*. London, Routledge.

O'Farrell, C. (2005). *Michel Foucault*. London, Sage.

O'Leary, T. (2002). *Foucault and the art of ethics*. London, Continuum.

Peters, M. A. and Besley, T. (eds) (2007). *Why Foucault? New directions in educational research*. New York, Peter Lang.

Popkewitz, T. S. and Brennan, M. (1997). Restructuring of social and political theory in education: Foucault and a social epistemology of school practices. *Educational Theory*, 47 (3), 287–313.

Popkewitz, T. S. and Brennan, M. (eds) (1998). *Foucault's challenge: Discourse, knowledge, and power in education*. New York, Teachers College Press.

Scott, J. C. (1985). *Weapons of the weak: Everyday forms of peasant resistance*. London, Yale University Press.

Scott, J. C. (1990). *Domination and the art of resistance: Hidden transcripts*. London, Yale University Press.

Townley, B. (1993). Foucault, power/knowledge and its relevance for human resource management. *Academy of Management Review*, 18 (3), 518–545.

Usher, R. and Edwards, R. (1994). *Postmodernism and education*. London and New York, Routledge.

Weedon, C. (1987). *Feminist practice and poststructuralist theory*. Oxford, Basil Blackwell.

4 Ridgeway State High School
Articulating a telos of social justice

So, I think I've really been able to define social justice for me as a person in the last seven months, for the first time in my career really. And maybe that's a sad indictment on the opportunities I've had in life.

(Carol)

Ridgeway State High School is situated in a very poor urban area of Queensland, Australia. For the last few decades the school has had a troubled history of violence, a high turnover of staff, poor attendance and low achievement. While Ridgeway has its own 'thisness' (Thomson, 2002) and particular history, it is a school that shares a number of concerns with others in similarly disadvantaged areas in many other parts of the world. Stories of poverty and disadvantage, violence and underachievement are common in many parts of the United States, the UK and Australia. Therefore, we hope that this case study will resonate with readers' experiences in their own schools. We think the sharing and theorising of such narratives will help to explain the complexities of leadership in these types of schools so that new and alternative strategies can be found to alleviate these issues and generate viable recommendations for policy-makers.

In this chapter we build a narrative of Carol, Ridgeway's principal, and her work in trying to deal with the significant challenges that a school like Ridgeway State High presents. We begin with the same quote that opened the book because it illustrates a key challenge for Carol: how her current position has led to major personal and professional reflection over what constitutes social justice. For Carol, context plays a key role in formulating responses to social justice issues and problems, and leadership can be constituted only through and by these particular contexts. Drawing on Foucault's fourfold ethical framework that we outlined in Chapter 3, we highlight the different practices Carol undertakes on herself as a principal working towards a particular telos of herself as leader, of social justice and of the school. Inherent in these practices is the constitution of herself as an advocate for redressing disadvantage (Anderson, 2009) while also being seen to comply with the high-stakes forms of accountability and managerialism that permeate the education policy landscape in Queensland as well as at a federal level throughout Australia (as outlined in Chapter 2). We work with Foucault's notion of subjectivity as it opens a space for identifying practices of resistance to performative, neoliberal accountabilities (Ball and Olmedo, 2013) in Carol's daily work. We believe that this is a key aspect in the work that educational leaders must do in order to pursue the goals of social justice and equity.

Carol's story will resonate with other principals in disadvantaged and diverse school settings. The tools that Foucault provides allow for a close examination of the moral and ethical dilemmas facing leaders of disadvantaged schools in the pursuit of social justice. We believe that Carol is doing some excellent work in this pursuit. However, the aim here is not to articulate what a politics of social justice should look like for educational leaders, but rather to explore the tensions and subjectivity or ethical self-formation of the subject implicit in these practices. We begin by providing an introductory portrait of the school, followed by an explanation of the research background and processes from which to understand the data presented in this chapter. The second part of this chapter draws explicitly on Foucault's notion of telos to analyse both the leadership telos of Carol as an individual principal and the telos of social justice being constructed throughout the school and shaped within broader modes of subjection. Then, in Chapter 5, we detail the forms of elaboration that are key to pursuing this telos: namely, practices of advocacy, truth-telling and counter-conduct.

Portrait of Ridgeway State High School

When one sees Ridgeway for the first time, one is immediately aware of the two-metre-high steel perimeter fence and the modern administration block, which contrast with the school building's traditional brick architecture and wooden, Queenslander-style verandah. This somewhat staid and conventional school front to the public is vastly different from what one might expect, given Ridgeway's troubled and difficult history. The permanently allocated police parking space outside the front of the administration block is a reminder of the school's not too distant past, when every window would be boarded up and fights between students were a daily occurrence. The part of Queensland in which the school is situated is well known for its high level of poverty and often tense relations between different Indigenous, Islander, Vietnamese and numerous other cultural groups.

In terms three and four of 2012, after Carol had stressed that significant refurbishment and building work were essential if Ridgeway were to remain viable, the school received a huge amount of funding under the State Schools of Tomorrow initiative. This paid for total refurbishment of a campus whose future had been in serious doubt. The installation of a suite of twenty-four-hour video cameras, including heat sensors, has resulted in a form of ongoing surveillance that at first glance could invoke apoplexy in a Foucauldian scholar. However, the principal and staff insist that this system (along with swipe-card access to administration and face-recognition cameras at reception) seems to have provided not only much needed security but also a marked improvement in student behaviour. The school also now employs security staff, plus two large Rottweiler dogs for night-time and special events.

Carol explains:

> If you came to this school prior to term three [in 2012], you would see that every single window in the whole school was boarded up. So there wasn't any light or fresh air going into the classrooms at all. The minute a window would be replaced it would be smashed that weekend. So, as part of State Schools of Tomorrow, the big fence right around the perimeter of the school was funded, I think for $90,000, and the whole school was refurbished. Part of the refurbishment and part of the requests that we made was that we would have pivotal video cameras, twenty-four-hour surveillance cameras, put in across the school. There are eighteen [of them], plus an additional ten that are fake. So there are eighteen that are in operation and anyone such as myself or the deputy principals can see from our desktop [video feeds from] those eighteen cameras around the school. So we can see the kids twenty-four/seven. We can also see their heat . . . They pick up the heat of the body as well, so at night-time, when we have a break-and-enter, we can see movement, a blue light movement on the camera, which we provide to the police, of course. [The cameras] have been absolutely outstanding. They have cut out bullying massively. The fence has stopped the entries on the weekend, and the amount of money we [have to] spend on fixing and getting rid of vandalism and graffiti and so forth has been cut by hundreds and hundreds and hundreds of per cent.

Of course, one could draw on Foucault's work to build a significant analysis of these practices of surveillance and panoptic gaze (see Foucault, 1977; Niesche, 2011), but that is not our primary focus in this case study. Carol is very quick to point out that students are shown footage of any indiscretion and that there are no cameras in the classrooms. She also stresses that both staff and students are happy with the new system:

> Students report feeling much safer and report feeling very comfortable with the cameras. If we do have an incident, we sit the student in front of the camera and say, 'Here's where you've taken your shirt off and pursued the other person. Can you see the evidence that we have?' That very quickly spreads across the school: 'If we do the wrong thing, then part of the evidence that contributes to any decision-making around consequences is that surveillance.' Teachers are very comfortable with it. They have not complained at all about being, you know, under surveillance; not at all. There's no surveillance in classrooms and mobile phones are not allowed at school at all. So there's no risk of staff being taped or filmed. It's just really for movement between classes, lunchtimes, but as I said it has contributed to a drastic drop in bullying, antisocial behaviours. And students and staff, you know, report feeling much safer.

On meeting Carol for the first time, she is immediately approachable and friendly, and very willing to 'show off' the recent changes at Ridgeway. With a school population of 430–450 students, one might be forgiven for asking, 'Where are the rest of the students?' as the grounds could easily accommodate twice that number. The students who are there are very happy to say hello as we walk around the school, looking at the serene grounds and buildings. It is difficult to picture the recent, much-publicised tension between groups of Pacific Islander and Indigenous students in the local community, as all the students we meet seem settled and happy.

Ridgeway's students are drawn from very linguistically and culturally diverse backgrounds. In total, twenty-four different nationalities are currently represented at the school. All of the students reside in a catchment area that is in the lowest socio-economic status quartile, with 90 per cent of them situated in the poverty bracket and 40 per cent from single-parent families. Long-term generational and situational poverty among these families leaves the students under-resourced and marginalised as learners. They have significant English-as-a-second-language needs but no additional or targeted funding is provided to meet these needs. However, as mentioned in Chapter 2, as the school is a National Partnership school, it has been accorded extra funding to lift its students' level of achievement.

Historically, the school has been well known as a challenging environment, with a high turnover of staff and leaders, and poor attendance remains a significant ongoing problem. NAPLAN results are still below the national average in all areas. The school currently employs around fifty teaching staff (both full and part time) and an additional forty support staff, including cleaners, administrative staff, teacher aides, Indigenous education workers and so on. As a result, just managing and looking after the staff involves a huge workload. The complexities of human resources for a school like this are also prevalent because, while Ridgeway is a state school, many of the staff (and particularly the support staff) are not from the Queensland state education department, which creates logistical headaches for Carol in her day-to-day business.

Carol was appointed principal in 2010 and tasked with lifting the school's performance with respect to national performance benchmarks. As principal of a National Partnership school, she was promised both a personal financial incentive (cash bonus) and more direct control over staffing if the school improved its performance against these benchmarks. The school was also promised significant extra funding if it achieved its targets. While these incentives were and continue to be seen as positives for the school, they have resulted in significant extra complexity for Carol. As part of the National Partnership school arrangements, she is employed on rolling six-month contracts; and if the school fails to reach its targets, her current contract can be terminated with only four weeks' notice. Clearly, then, the principal is playing for very high stakes whenever the school's test results are assessed!

In addition, the introduction of *MySchool* has created further challenges for Carol due to forms of accountability and the 'tyranny of transparency' (Strathern, 2000). Underperforming schools and schools in disadvantaged communities have found this new environment especially challenging (Lingard, 2010). The principal and senior staff are aware of these issues and have been working hard to change some teachers' deficit understandings of students that have been pervasive throughout the school for a number of years. Some of these issues are apparent in the interviews that are presented later in this chapter and in Chapter 5.

Locating the research

The data for this chapter and the next come from one school site that formed part of a much larger research project. While we do not wish to get bogged down in elaborate and lengthy descriptions of research methods and processes, we feel it is important to outline some of the main foundations upon which this research project and the one discussed in Chapters 6 and 7 are based.

This project had as its central aim to improve understanding of the complexities of school leadership that worked towards alleviating educational disadvantage among disadvantaged groups. The research consisted of a comparative case study of three schools in Queensland,

Australia, one of which was Ridgeway. From the outset we acknowledged the importance of school leadership in addressing issues of social justice, but we also accepted that we knew little about the day-to-day realities of working in disadvantaged contexts and the challenges for leaders in these schools as they felt and experienced them. The project sought to understand the constraints and possibilities of action in different school contexts and also to identify practices that were addressing issues of social justice. The specific research questions included:

- How do principals enact social justice in their schools?
- What are the constraints in their work towards social justice?
- How do principals respond to and address these constraints?
- How can these work practices be theorised to improve understanding of the competing subjectivities of principals advocating for social justice?

Elements of productive leadership (Hayes et al., 2004; Niesche and Keddie, 2011) as well as advocacy leadership (Anderson, 2009) were important for the framing of the research project.

As stated, the research project adopted a comparative case study approach consisting of multiple qualitative dimensions, including interviews, observations and school document analysis. The three schools were invited to participate based upon their recognised commitment to addressing issues of equity and disadvantage. The research project was conducted over three years and in that time each school was visited on a number of occasions, with interviews undertaken with approximately twelve members of staff in each school, in addition to four extended interviews with each principal. As the project was primarily concerned with the work and constraints of school principals, these formed the majority of the data collected and also the majority of the data used in this and subsequent chapters. It is important to note here that we do not consider leadership to be the preserve of just the principal, as teaching staff, administrative staff, parents, students and community groups and members all play key roles too in various aspects of daily school life. While we focus predominantly on the leadership of one principal, our intention is not to underplay the significance of leadership at other levels in the school or the work of teachers and other staff. We focus on Carol's story simply to illuminate the complexities of that particular role and how she undertakes particular practices of the self. Our interview questions were framed around exploring individual and school philosophies of social justice, leadership, the challenges of working in disadvantaged schools and the practices and strategies that are employed to overcome these challenges.

The analysis of data presented in this chapter draws on Foucault's ethical framework. In particular, we outline a telos of the principal, in terms of the sort of leader Carol aspires to be, followed by an articulation of a telos of social justice employed not only by Carol but by other staff within the school. Throughout the chapter, we locate this telos – and, more specifically, Carol's attempts to adopt an ethical approach to leading her school – within the broader modes of subjection shaping education in Queensland.

A telos of leadership

There are numerous discourses surrounding and comprising the work of school principals. Multiple and often conflicting discourses construct the principal and principalship in diverse and complex ways (Gillies, 2013; Lingard et al., 2003; Niesche, 2011). The field of educational leadership has sought to describe and capture what good leadership and effective principals are through the drafting of various leadership models, leadership and principal standards, and school effectiveness and improvement literatures. As we discussed in Chapter 2, while there is an increasing body of literature examining leadership and issues of social justice (as well as a recent education policy focus), there remains a lack of in-depth studies of leadership for social justice that examine what leaders actually do in their day-to-day work, and how this forms the ethical subject, practices of resistance and care of the self. As we show in the next chapter, Carol works with and against these discourses as forms of elaboration, but they also play a significant role in a telos of how she sees the kind of principal and kind of subject she wishes to be.

The role of the principal is undoubtedly one that is both moral and ethical. In Foucault's terms, 'moral' refers to a set of values or rules of action that are prescribed by particular agencies, organisations, cultural norms and so on. For a school principal, these could be education department standards, guides and principles or they could be religiously based for some independent and Catholic schools. For Foucault, 'ethics' refers to the behaviours of individuals in relation to these moral codes (Foucault, 1992). The important aspect of this is the way in which an individual acts, responds and conducts herself/himself. In other words, ethics is the relationship one has with oneself. For Carol, as principal of Ridgeway, this means how she acts, conducts herself and works within the prescribed code of action and behaviour set out by the education department, but also how she attempts to meet the expectations of the local community. This is a political space where her forms of elaboration and modes of subjection lie (these are explored in the next chapter).

We take the 'telos of the principal' to mean the type of principal and/or leader Carol sees as being characteristic of the ethical subject she wishes to be, and one that is needed to improve the school and student outcomes. This is not about prescribing a particular mode of being or way of acting, a particular fixed identity of 'the leader' or the principal. Rather, it is a more fluid, contradictory subject positioning that shifts and changes according to the various demands placed upon Carol by both herself and the school. For instance, Carol describes how the strategies she employed in her previous school would be inappropriate at Ridgeway:

> Personally . . . I'm having to develop a whole new set of new strategies that I've never had to think about using before. So, the strategies that I guess have become second nature and I established early in my deputy principalship and my principalship don't work here. I guess I felt disempowered when I first started. I thought, 'Oh my God, what am I going to do? How do you do this?'

By 'strategies', Carol means the particular practices she uses that represent a particular 'style of leadership'. Rather than attempt to prescribe what type of leadership style Carol or other leaders should employ, we focus more on her perceptions, her telos and how she undertakes particular practices in the formation of herself as the ethical subject she aspires to be. This is intimately linked to the way in which Carol exercises power as principal and how she is used as a vehicle for the exercising of power by the state education authority, as well as to Carol's practices of resistance and counter-conduct that we explore in the next chapter.

The need to develop new strategies led Carol to reconsider her telos of the type of leader she wished to be and the types of practices and strategies she would employ at Ridgeway. Due to the particular school context and its challenges for Carol as the new principal, she recognised that she needed to work differently at different times and in response to different expectations from staff, students and parents. When asked to describe her 'leadership style', she responds:

> I've always seen myself as a very authoritarian leader and I think it's been relatively successful. And I guess I work from a premise, or have worked from a premise in the past, that young people need boundaries. But in the last couple of years I really have worked very hard at the distributed leadership model and that's also going very well. It's interesting because there are some great examples of distributed leadership in the school, and I really try to nurture them and prosper those as much as I can.

In the past, then, Carol was what she describes as an 'authoritarian leader', but at Ridgeway she has found that this particular subjectivity is sometimes less than effective. This may be due to her new environment, her level of experience, her age or some other factor. Hence, she has 'tried on' a distributed leadership way of being and found it to be largely successful. However, she remarks:

> But, you know, there are times . . . when community people, parents, students and teachers just want a decision, and they want a decision from you . . . At the end of the day, I'm the one accountable for those outcomes for these kids and at the end of the day somebody has to make a decision and say, 'You know what? This is what we're going to do.' So I think I've learned a lot about myself as a person and as a leader. And I think I am changing and that, as the years go by, I probably will become less authoritarian. I probably will become more and more confident and more and more empowering of others, and I think generally we will move that way. Having said that, the instructional leadership model that our leaders are espousing . . . probably . . . contests some of those thoughts. So . . . I don't think that I'm any one particular leader. I think I've drawn on a range of leadership styles. And certainly in the first couple of months of a new school, I think you probably use the authoritarian leadership position the most. As you become more comfortable, you develop your teams, and you become more focused about what the intentions are and what the plan is. I think you move away. Then a crisis happens and you find yourself back into that . . . very authoritarian or instructional mode.

Carol is familiar with a range of leadership literature, having completed a Masters of Education (Leadership). She understands the models and the jargon, so she is able to frame her telos as a leader in those frames. She easily inserts terms such as 'distributed leadership', 'instructional leadership' and 'authoritarian leadership' when discussing her own leadership. In a way, the leadership literature is acting here as a discursive norm, or mode of subjection, according to which Carol modifies her behaviour and actions. Carol's leadership is a form of ethical substance on which she works in order to be the type of principal she wants to be, that is a telos of the principal. This is a different way of theorising leadership from the traditional models and approaches. Articulating leadership as a form of ethical substance allows it to be positioned as a shifting subject positioning in relation to the other aspects of Foucault's fourfold framework. This allows a more nuanced reading of the ways that principals work towards a particular telos by 'working on' their leadership in various ways. It is not a matter of being a particular type of leader; rather, the practices enacted on the self towards that telos are important. Leadership then becomes one frame of many that make up a telos of social justice in schools, one that is heavily dependent on, and in fact constructed according to, the school context and various modes of subjection.

The above extracts from interviews with Carol are illustrative of the multiple and competing discourses at work in her subjectivity as principal (and probably those of many other principals). There is no one way of working; instead, there is a constant shifting and changing of one's telos based on circumstances, the demands of the school context and Carol's formation of her own subjectivity as the type of leader she wishes to be. This is where Foucault's notion of subjectivity can provide a different way of thinking about and theorising the leadership practices of principals through recognising leadership as an ongoing process of construction, re-construction and renegotiation. As Foucault (2000: 290) says, the subject is not a substance but a form. Ball and Olmedo (2013: 87; emphasis in original) also draw on this notion when they argue:

> This perspective allows us to approach the idea of subjectivity as *processes of becoming* that focus on *what we do* rather than *what we are*, that is to say, the work of the care of the self. The point here is that no individual, no self, is ontologically prior to power. There is no subject that is already formed. In this sense, the self is not only a constant *beginning* but also a constant *end*.

Interestingly, Carol also explicitly refers to the notion of servant leadership (Greenleaf, 1977) when she describes her leadership and underlying beliefs:

> I take very seriously the whole service position that I'm in and the fact that I am a government officer that's reporting to a community and servicing a community . . . And there's a sense of pride that comes with the job that you do. Particularly in tough situations, you know . . . particularly as a principal and even as a deputy principal in large schools, for example a very large school of 1550, often you're the last opportunity to make a difference for somebody. Often you're the last stop to resolve an issue and that's a very humbling position to be in, I guess. And . . . it's nice to take that position seriously and to do what you can to assist, you know?

Broadly sitting under the umbrella of ethical leadership, servant leadership is about service to followers and is concerned with nurturing, defending and empowering others (Yukl, 2002). Carol talks of being the last stop in terms of making a difference for disadvantaged students and communities. Elements of servant leadership certainly do come through in interviews with teachers at Ridgeway when they are asked about Carol's leadership. One could also argue that there could be elements of other leadership models, such as distributed, collaborative, reciprocal and so on. Such is the fallacy of attempting to define and categorise leadership according to these models, for leadership at times may be all or none of them. The usefulness of these labels is therefore severely limited. Some of the responses from teachers concerning Carol's leadership are presented below:

> Very consistent. We know where we stand, high expectations, transparent, collaborative ... she's creating and giving you the opportunity to learn from others. So, just a very open leadership model, I think. Very supportive, caring, you know, all of those things. So, yeah, fantastic. Committed as well is something because I've been here for ... eight years and I think I've seen about seven principals. So to have someone that's committed to our school under the National Partnership is absolutely fantastic . . . There's a definite feel of stability in the school and she offers that, so, yeah ... she's definitely positive.
>
> (Teacher 1)

> She's very ... honest, she's open, she's an excellent communicator, she's clear in what she wants, and staff here are very much aware of what her expectation is. She is committed and she's very aware. She's not one of these principals that likes to stick their head in a paper bag and not think about what's happening out there. You know, she's done her research on the community and she knows what this community needs and she believes this is a community school, it's not her school. It's the community's school, and that's a big difference. Most principals think, 'This is my school and what I want for this school . . .' But her vision is 'What does the community need from this school?'
>
> (Teacher 2)

> I think that Carol is a really dynamic leader. It's very clear what her expectations are. She's very good at fostering leadership within other people and inspiring them. She's very good at recognising what you do, sometimes to the point where I think, 'Is she just saying that ... to recognise it or does she really think you've done a good job?' So ... that ... is probably something that I'm not sure of.

But, you know, it's better than somebody that puts you down all the time, isn't it?

(Teacher 3)

I think she likes to know everything that's going on but she doesn't necessarily feel that she has to do it all herself. I think she's very good at . . . helping people to find their strengths and putting them in positions where they can use those strengths. She's very good at mentoring people. And you can see that there's a genuine care for her staff, which I think people appreciate. And she doesn't expect anything from anybody else that she wouldn't do herself.

(Teacher 4)

A number of themes emerged from these interviews. The teachers repeatedly used terms such as 'consistent', 'committed', 'transparent', 'excellent communicator' and 'supportive' to describe both Carol's leadership itself and her leadership practices. While it would be easy to draw up a list of characteristics from these descriptions to develop a model of good leadership, this would lead to a closing down of the dialogue about leadership practices in challenging contexts rather than an opening up of debates about models and practices that are developed through particular locations and intersections of culture, society and history in Carol's leadership at Ridgeway. It is important to remember that subjectivity is a site of struggle and resistance (Ball and Olmedo, 2013) and that Carol's leadership is dynamic, responsive and multifaceted. Rather than seeing her leadership as any particular notion of leadership or model, Foucault's work allows us to see and theorise the principal as subject as an ongoing construction of identities. Carol is in a constant process of 'becoming' principal or leader, and this is the strength of her leadership. By exploring her practices of self-formation as principal, as she demonstrates, leadership is not a static concept.

The perceptions of Carol's leadership as illustrated in the above comments from Ridgeway's teachers illustrate the huge diversity of her appreciated characteristics and actions. These subjectivities are sites of struggle for Carol and are heavily impacted upon and constructed through a range of factors. Foucault (2000: 291) notes that 'practices of the self are not invented by the individual but are proposed, suggested and imposed upon him by culture, society and societal group'. Therefore, these terms used by the teachers are not simply characteristics of Carol as a person, as a leader; rather, they are found and developed in relation to these complex factors, in the same way as a telos of social justice is determined. We turn to this in the next section.

A telos of social justice

When talking to Carol, it soon becomes apparent that her view of social justice and of being principal of a school like Ridgeway involves particular types of work and telos. However, her views have not come without any self-reflection, internal turmoil and a preparedness to change her beliefs. She often remarks on how her previous views have been challenged by working at Ridgeway. For instance:

> I think my view of social justice has probably changed in the last seven months, to be honest. Having grown up in . . . a very working-class community, attending a working-class school, but from parents and an extended family of middle-class values and very much a middle-class family, I'd made a lot of assumptions up until the last seven months about social justice. But in the last seven months, I very passionately feel and very strongly feel that social justice is about the fact that where you grew up and what your background is culturally or, you know, your family background, your socio-economic background, regardless of what your history is and what your background is, it shouldn't determine how successful you are in life. And I guess I've really defined my view in the last seven months because I see and live it on a daily basis that if you are born in a particular postcode then 90 per cent of you will be unemployed, 97 per cent of you will live in a poverty situation . . . I haven't worked in Indigenous communities, but I did grow up in a community that was pretty tough. But it was a working-class community with many, many working-class infrastructures, such as the mines, the railway workshops and some good, strong family values and probably some strong church groups within the community, and, you know, strong foundations. Whereas this community is nothing like I've ever worked in before.

When asked to define her view of social justice further, Carol responds:

> Once I thought it was about opportunity . . . I dabbled with ideas [like] 'If we provide the opportunity [and] they don't take it up, well, bad luck. And that's probably a middle-class value system that I've inherited from my family. But now my understanding of social justice is far more sophisticated than that . . . And you know what, I'm not even sure that I thought about it too much, to be honest. But living and working and breathing in this community, it's not about opportunity. I mean, you can – I can – and you do throw relentless amounts of opportunity at one child or many children and they

simply don't take it up. Well, that's not social justice. So, I guess it's about removing the barriers. It's about belief. It's about continually being prepared to knock on the door and saying, 'Come on. Let's do this. You can do this. We can do this.'

These comments illustrate the tensions within Carol's own beliefs as she moved from some aspects of a deficit discourse to one of removing barriers and providing support to take up opportunities. Carol's telos of her role and the school is intertwined with these changing beliefs; and, as we discuss in the next chapter, the school has worked on her ethical self-formation as a mode of elaboration that is an aspect of her self-formation that she hadn't necessarily anticipated. This is where context matters in understanding educational leadership. Carol's leadership and work practices are co-constructed with her school context. Therefore, leadership is not a mode of adjectival behaviour or a characteristic that is implemented in a school; rather, leadership practices are implicitly developed with the school's cultural, economic and social history. In this way one could also see the school context acting as a mode of subjection on Carol's leadership practices and self-formation as a principal. This means that a telos is not fixed; it is in a constant state of evolution.

Given the specific contextual circumstances at Ridgeway, for Carol this means a social justice telos that is predominantly focused on removing the economic barriers impeding her students' capacity to participate on a par with their more privileged peers in more privileged schools (Fraser, 1997). The brief portrait of the school earlier in this chapter illuminates the significance of material or economic support for the school. Indeed, without the injection of funds from the State Schools of Tomorrow initiative, Ridgeway would no longer exist. This form of redistributive justice transformed the school from an unsafe and unwelcoming environment (where theft, vandalism and graffiti were prevalent) to a safe and more peaceful environment (where there is less bullying and fewer instances of antisocial behaviour). While one might question the high levels of policing that are required to maintain this safe environment, these changes have clearly addressed some of the economic conditions that are likely to curtail students' access to, and participation in, school life (Fraser, 1997).

The high levels of disadvantage arising from the poverty, crime and unemployment within the community can be seen as strengthening Carol's commitment to this redistributive justice focus towards breaking the link between poverty and success. As she says, 'your background . . . shouldn't determine how successful you are in life'. She is committed to ensuring her school is adequately resourced materially to begin ameliorating the conditions that create such disadvantage, and similarly committed to dismantling the deficit constructions of her students that often accompany such disadvantage (as noted at the beginning of this chapter). As she says, 'It's about belief [and] continually being prepared to [say], 'Let's do this. You can do this. We can do this.' In terms of social justice, this focus on high expectations is a major emphasis for other leaders at the school, as the director of student achievement explains:

> For me, social justice is the best teachers in all schools, because education is the key. So, for me, you know, apathy doesn't fall far from the tree so we need to really be role models for our students. So, social justice, for me, is making these kids believe that they can do this. My thing is, if I can make these kids believe they can do this, then they will start to push back on their teachers, and they will demand more of their teachers.

Clearly, then, the director of student achievement has a strong belief in high expectations of the teaching staff:

> And I think the other big challenge . . . is raising the awareness or the understanding of teachers that our kids can do this. Just because they're from Ridgeway, don't put them in a box. I have to admit the first couple of weeks I was here, people, teachers, were saying to me, 'Why are you working so hard? Our kids can't do this.' And I actually said to a teacher one day, 'Don't tell me "can't" and don't tell me "no".'

High expectations of students are key to working against the deficit understandings that lead to comments such as 'Our [i.e. underprivileged] kids can't do this [i.e. succeed at school]' (Lingard et al., 2003; Hayes et al., 2004, 2006). Akin to Carol's remarks about the significance of postcodes in determining students' future success in life, this is about recognising and challenging the correlations between student economic and social marginality, their lower educational attainment, their early school leaving and their future economic and social disadvantages. As noted in Chapter 2, education determines employment credentialing and students' subsequent access to the labour market (Connell, 1994; Mills and Gale, 2010; Keddie, 2012). Thus, a key platform of socially just schooling must be to prepare all students for their future productive participation within this market (Mills and Gale, 2010; Gerwitz et al., 1995).

This involves assisting marginalised or disadvantaged students to achieve on the 'same measuring sticks' of educational achievement as their more privileged counterparts so that they can 'eventually access society in the same way that any other [student] would' (see also Ladson-Billings, 1995; Sarra, 2003).

At Ridgeway, there is, of course, recognition of the significance of these external 'measuring sticks' or modes of subjection as indicators of the school's 'success' in educating students. This is reflected in the school's focus and improvement on these measures (i.e. standardised tests such as NAPLAN). There is also recognition of the narrowness of these performative technologies, especially as they are represented publicly in forums such as *MySchool*. This forum is seen as reinforcing deficit understandings of schools and communities through the public display of standardised test scores. During the interviews, the principal and teachers were all critical of the representation of Ridgeway through such mechanisms as *MySchool*. For example:

> To me, it doesn't adequately reflect the value add schools do. It has no avenue to report on the social, emotional value add . . . You know, if there was that function for us, we'd score out of sight . . . Because we will constantly be judged. We will always be judged on the academic outcomes of students, but I can guarantee you at the end of the day maybe our students won't achieve academically as best [or] as well as someone at Grammar or something, and I'm sure they could, but there are always going to be some . . . social barriers that will get in their way. That website will never measure the challenge we have [faced] to that social barrier and how we've conquered that social barrier. And that's where low socio-economic schools will always lose out because of that website.
>
> (Director of student achievement)

These comments reflect the feelings of all the staff at Ridgeway, who view the *MySchool* website as an example of how deficit discourses are entrenched through the public demonstration of school results in standardised tests. The elements of social and emotional support that are provided by the school, and are central aspects of its telos of social justice, cannot be measured on *MySchool*. Hence, they do not 'count' in terms of what the school produces and how its effectiveness is measured. As Harvey (2010: 192) says, 'only as recorded and public are we made real, and once recorded and publicized, what is real is hollowed and empty and leaves nary a trace'.

Despite the pressures of high-stakes accountability through mechanisms of performativity such as *MySchool*, the school and its staff are determined to focus on the things that matter to them and their students. This is an unwavering commitment led by Carol, and it is reflected in the elements comprising her telos as demonstrated throughout this chapter. These are all ethical situations that require the reflective practices of weighing up the needs of the students and community against formal hierarchical reporting, accountabilities and other modes of subjection. It is within these spaces that particular subjectivities are formed and constituted through various sets of power relations.

Conclusion

This chapter has introduced the case study of Ridgeway State High School and its principal, Carol. The background context of this school is key to understanding and analysing the leadership practices that are currently undertaken in the school. Ridgeway is a school that presents significant challenges for its principal and the rest of the leadership team, including aspects of long-term poverty, violence, abuse, poor housing and high ESL needs, to name a few. These challenges have led Carol to pursue a telos of social justice that she considers essential and central to her work as principal in order for good teaching and learning to occur. We have used Foucault's notion of telos – a part of his ethical framework – to show how this is a key aspect of the formation of Carol as an ethical subject. From here, it is possible to begin to analyse the practices that Carol and others in the school have instated to work towards this vision of what it means to be a good principal and improved outcomes for the school and its students.

In the next chapter, we explore the practices of advocacy, truth-telling and counter-conduct at Ridgeway. Within the context of a disadvantaged community, and the demands of state and federal governments, we focus on the significance of these practices in Carol's pursuit of socially just leadership and overcoming the vast challenges this school presents.

References

Anderson, G. (2009). *Advocacy leadership: Toward a post-reform agenda in education.* London and New York, Routledge.

Ball, S. J. and Olmedo, A. (2013). Care of the self, resistance and subjectivity under neoliberal governmentalities. *Critical Studies in Education*, 54 (1), 85–96.

Chubbuck, S. (2010). Individual and structural orientations in socially just teaching: Conceptualization, implementation, and collaborative effort. *Journal of Teacher Education*, 61 (3), 197–210.

Connell, R. (1994). Poverty and education. *Harvard Educational Review*, 64, 125–149.

Foucault, M. (1977). *Discipline and punish.* New York, Pantheon Books.

Foucault, M. (1992). *The history of sexuality*, Volume II: *The use of pleasure.* Harmondsworth, Penguin.

Foucault, M. (2000). The ethics of the concern for self as a practice of freedom. In. P. Rabinow (ed.) *Essential works of Foucault 1954–1984*, Volume I: *Ethics*. London, Penguin.

Fraser, N. (1997). *Justice interruptus: Critical reflections on the 'postsocialist' condition*. New York, Routledge.

Gerwitz, S., Ball, S. J., and Bowe, R. (1995). *Markets, choice, and equity in education*. Buckingham, Open University Press.

Gillies, D. (2013). *Educational leadership and Michel Foucault*. London and New York, Routledge.

Greenleaf, R. K. (1977). *Servant leadership: A journey into the nature of legitimate power and greatness*. New York, Paulist Press.

Harvey, C. (2010). Making hollow men. *Educational Theory*, 60 (2), 189–201.

Hayes, D., Christie, P., Mills, M. and Lingard, R. (2004). Productive leaders and productive leadership. *Journal of Educational Administration*, 42 (5), 520–538.

Hayes, D., Mills, M., Christie, P. and Lingard, R. (2006). *Teachers and schooling making a difference*. Crows Nest, Allen and Unwin.

Keddie, A. (2012). *Educating for diversity and social justice*. New York, Routledge.

Knight, J. (1994). Social justice and effective schooling. *Education Views*, 3 (8), 8.

Ladson-Billings, G. (1995). Toward a theory of culturally relevant pedagogy. *American Educational Research Journal*, 32 (3), 465–491.

Lingard, R. (2010). Policy borrowing, policy learning: Testing times in Australian schooling. *Critical Studies in Education*, 51 (2), 129–147.

Lingard, R., Hayes, D., Mills, M. and Christie, P. (2003). *Leading learning*. Maidenhead, Open University Press.

McConaghy, C. (2000). *Rethinking Indigenous education: Culturalism, colonialism and the politics of knowing*. Flaxton, Post Pressed.

Mills, C. and Gale, T. (2010). *Schooling in disadvantaged communities: Playing the game from the back of the field*. Dordrecht, Springer.

Niesche, R. (2011). *Foucault and educational leadership: Disciplining the principal*. London, Routledge.

Niesche, R. and Keddie, A. (2011). Foregrounding issues of equity and diversity in educational leadership. *School Leadership and Management*, 31 (1), 65–77.

Sarra, C. (2003). *Cherbourg State School, strong and smart, What Works program: Improving outcomes for Indigenous students*. From www.whatworks.edu.au/dbAction.do?cmd=displaySitePage1andsubcmd=selectandid=111, accessed 11 March 2015.

Strathern, M. (2000). The tyranny of transparency. *British Educational Research Journal*, 26 (3), 309–321.

Thomson, P. (2002). *Schooling the rustbelt kids: Making the difference in changing times*. Crows Nest, Allen and Unwin.

Yukl, G. (2002). *Leadership in organizations*, 5th edition. Upper Saddle River, NJ, Prentice-Hall.

5 Advocacy, truth-telling and counter-conduct as practices of socially just leadership at Ridgeway

In this chapter we outline the particular practices that Carol undertakes in the pursuit of her telos of social justice. We explore the ethical substance of her leadership (outlined briefly in the previous chapter) that she works on as a technique of the self. Further to this, we illustrate the modes of subjection that lead Carol to act in particular ways. These include the various leadership discourses, policies from the education authorities, the expectations from community and parents as well as the high needs of the students at Ridgeway. In addition to these, we reflect on the forms of elaboration, or practices of self-formation, that form her work. We argue that a significant part of Carol's work involves advocacy for her students and the different ways in which she undertakes practices of counter-conduct. Another aspect of Carol's advocacy work is the notion of parrhesia or truth-telling (discussed in Chapter 3), which, for Carol, is a key element in her self-formation as principal. Interestingly, she also employs an active form of silenced discourse around some issues, such as her accountability as a principal in relation to standards documents and the controversial *MySchool* website.

The chapter is divided largely into the thematic work that constitutes Carol's forms of elaboration: namely, advocacy, truth-telling and counter-conduct. We describe and explain the modes of subjection throughout each section.

Social justice leadership practices

The work that Carol does is informed by her telos of social justice and herself as principal that we outlined in the previous chapter. Her forms of elaboration consist of a range of activities and practices that have, at their core, a commitment to Carol's particular ethos of equity and social justice. These are not just about her own individual beliefs, but are particular to the school, its context and her position as school principal. As 'head' of the school, the principal is directly accountable for performance outcomes and reporting to the education department and other stakeholders. Annual reviews, desktop audits, grant applications, results in national testing regimes such as NAPLAN and the publishing of those results on *MySchool* all work to render principals accountable, disciplined and perpetually assessable subjects (Deleuze, 1992; Foucault, 1977). Nikolas Rose (1990) also refers to how one is rendered accountable and calculable according to the needs of different sets of stakeholders. Lingard (2012) emphasises the importance of policy by numbers in these policy shifts, and how data can work as a catalyst that can have perverse effects (Lingard and Sellar, 2013). These neoliberal modes of governmental rationality also work as powerful modes of subjection. As Dardot and Laval (2013) argue, in these forms of neoliberalism the subject is always to be constructed. Governmentality, in its neoliberal form, makes conducting others through the subject's own conduct one of its primary goals. For Carol, as principal, this results in a tension between being accountable to stakeholders such as Education Queensland (EQ) and parents through the access granted to them via *MySchool*, and her opportunities to engage with a broader or more holistic notion of what social justice means to her in a complex low SES community. These are central to her positioning as a particular type of subject. She acknowledges this tension between measuring outcomes, such as test scores, and her other important social and political work, which is much more difficult to 'measure':

> It is very much focused on literacy and numeracy outcomes. There is some focus to a lesser extent on social outcomes. I'm not sure how that's measured . . . We can measure what's happening in classrooms and the outcomes. How do I measure the work that I'm doing at a bigger level?

In this era of high-stakes testing and performance accountabilities, often only what can be measured is deemed important. And, indeed, Carol understands that part of her role is to report on performance benchmarks and measurable outcomes. However, other significant aspects of her work – which she feels are at least as important as this reporting – are difficult or even impossible to measure. She goes on to explain what she means by the 'bigger level':

> Some of the big issues I have to grapple with are the issues that are much bigger than education. I would say that . . . educating these students is a massive issue but it sits within a much bigger and more complex world of poverty, of housing, of food, of accommodation, of a network of people that care and support the young person, a

world of abuse, a world of domestic violence, a world of criminality is a big one . . . So there is a whole range of issues that are bigger than me that are impacting so significantly on education like I've never experienced in any other school I've been in.

These, then, are the issues that affect Carol's everyday work practices in the school. Factors such as poverty, housing, food, violence and criminality impact upon the day-to-day teaching and learning of Ridgeway's students, and providing these students with the care and support they need is imperative but also impossible to measure against educational performance benchmarks. Moreover, these factors are specific to Ridgeway and rarely encountered in schools that achieve high results on standardised tests and top the rankings on the *MySchool* website. The high needs of the students act as modes of subjection for Carol, as these are direct factors in her leadership work. These are the needs that drive her advocacy and her work in becoming a political subject. She recalls having to bite her tongue when someone from the education department informed her that 'postcode doesn't matter'. It is her students' needs that have forced Carol to recognise her obligations to them and the community, rather than a direct mandate from above in the form of state and/or federal education policy. Michael Fullan (1993: 22) famously argued that 'you can't mandate what matters', and in this case it seems to be indicative of the drivers leading to particular leadership work for Carol in her school context. What matters, for Ridgeway's students, cannot be mandated from above. Their needs, and those of their local community, as modes of subjection, have made Carol realise her commitment to social justice. Those needs include alleviating high levels of disadvantage and marginalisation.

The principal as advocate or 'political subject'

It is at this 'bigger level' where Carol is constructing herself as a political subject, having to profile and address issues that she terms 'bigger than education'. She clearly feels that her work is highly political, and she is constantly engaging with the contested terrain of meeting performance benchmarks, following the expectations of the state education authorities, and delivering the appropriate level of care in terms of emotional and social support for the students and the community in the pursuit of equity and social justice. At Ridgeway, care from the staff is delivered amid high expectations from both students and other members of staff, and practical support is provided through counselling with an understanding of the difficult situations of many of the school's students in terms of long-term situational poverty and the other 'bigger' issues Carol mentioned. Every teacher we interviewed mentioned the high level of care for the students at the school. The following two extracts are illustrative of their responses:

> I've been in a lot of schools, and I've taught in the western suburbs of Sydney, [and] this school is the best school I have ever seen at looking after students. This school genuinely cares for the students like I have never seen before and it is beautiful. It is just so supportive and I've been waiting my whole teaching life so far to find a school that cares for students so much ... You don't get rapped over the knuckles for caring for your students [here], whereas, in a lot of schools I've been in, it was like there was a line and you don't step over the line. Well, it's so nice to see that some staff here are prepared to step over that line. That's something that this school does very, very well.
>
> (Teacher 1)

> I think we're really, really good at supporting our students ... We have a really good, caring, nurturing staff here that works together really well for the best for the students.
>
> (Teacher 2)

The work done by Carol and the rest of Ridgeway's staff includes practices that cannot be measured or captured by standardised test scores or the data published on *MySchool*. They are in the difficult position of having to decide how much time and energy to devote to these aspects of their work and how much to spend on the other, more quantifiable aspects that are demanded by current reporting and accountability mandates. These are ethical decisions that Carol must negotiate in response to the students' and the community's needs. In what follows, she explains the tension she feels in terms of meeting the expectations of both the community and the state government, which is currently pushing principals to be 'curriculum leaders':

> If you look at any week, I guess it says a lot about the leadership in a place like this because sometimes I feel like a bit of a politician. You know, it's about working with the different factions and the different constituents. [You have to] ... hear, listen, respond to all of the different constituents' needs. And I think that snapshot of a diary ... gives a really good indication of how much time I'm probably not spending in classrooms, leading learning. I'm not suggesting that I'm not leading learning, but I guess I'm leading learning from a higher view or a broader view, which is a little bit in opposition to the expectations of Education Queensland at the moment.

Here, Carol freely acknowledges that she may not be leading learning in the manner prescribed by the state's education department – that is, she is not necessarily conforming to the department's view of principals as curriculum and instructional leaders. However, she has weighed this against the importance of meeting the expectations and needs of her staff, students, parents and local community members – her other 'constituents'. Carol's comments indicate that there is a tension between the needs of these various constituents. They are all modes of subjection, but Carol has to decide which mode she will act upon at any given time, and she has made a conscious decision to try to meet the needs of students and parents first, rather than subscribe to the pervasive audit culture at the expense of other issues. However, it is important to recognise that Carol portrays these modes of subjection as a binary. Some elements of the audit culture serve some parents' and students' needs; and many principals have welcomed standardised testing, such as NAPLAN, especially in its diagnostic capacity to direct appropriate support and resources to underperforming cohorts of students. While this does little to problematise the underlying priorities of these tests, such diagnosis nevertheless supports students to achieve on the 'measuring sticks' that count (Sarra, 2003).

How to act in relation to these various modes of subjection involves highly ethical decisions that form Carol's subjectivity in particular ways. Ethics and politics are inseparable (Dardot and Laval, 2013). Carol expresses how she feels 'like a bit of a politician' not only through her words but through her actions, as is demonstrated below. She actively constitutes herself as a political subject as principal. For example, her use of terms like 'constituents' indicates that she has adopted this form of subjectivity. She still believes she is 'leading learning', but from a different subject position from what she perceives is required of someone in her role by Education Queensland in a more formal instructional leadership capacity. She recognises that her leadership is a form of ethical substance that needs 'working on' in order to achieve her telos and become the type of principal she wishes to be. This could also be seen as an example of what Foucault (2007) terms counter-conduct. (We provide more examples of this later in the chapter.)

By articulating her job as approximating that of a politician, Carol is opening up a space for contestation and resistance that allows her to 'take on' some of the expectations placed on her by Education Queensland. However, she is also able to resist these expectations and create space for other issues that she thinks are important, such as the explicit philosophy of caring for and supporting the students emotionally. This is where resistance is not only productive but intrinsic to the functioning of governmentality (Foucault, 1991). The formation of the principal as political subject emerges within these spaces, as Carol negotiates her way through the tensions between the different discourses (what is prescribed by Education Queensland, her own telos as an ethical subject, and the expectations of Ridgeway's staff and students). As Foucault (2002: 342) points out, 'power is exercised over subjects, only insofar as they are free': that is, individuals are placed in circumstances in which they have various possibilities to act, and they are open to certain modes of conduct (or counter-conduct) or behaviours. It is in these spaces where individuals are constituted as particular subjects. For example, Carol is trying to alter long-existing perceptions among the community and students:

> It's the social checking that I have to do myself that I have to keep working hard and instilling in the staff that this is not OK. And to what extent are our practices and our beliefs reinstilling, exacerbating, and not challenging the status of this community? I have rearticulated an agenda and ensured that we are focused on learning, and I'm challenging social justice issues rather than reinforcing, you know, some of those social issues here.

Here, Carol is rearticulating an agenda of high expectations that she believes has not been present in some teachers and parts of the local community for some time. She has made it clear to teachers and staff that low expectations and deficit thinking towards students must change, along with a rigorous curriculum. She also states in interviews that the system has let down these students and their community, and that she is working to change that status quo. This is due to long-standing factors such as the perpetuation of deficit understandings of students in poverty and Indigenous students, along with the more recent privileging of a narrow culture of standards and auditing that further marginalises and entrenches deficit thinking in the community. She is actively seeking to disrupt the existing levels of low expectations around student achievement. She has expressed concern about the long-term underperformance of the community, and has articulated a sense of capacity to change and improve the situation. As she says:

> The issue is sustainability around National Partnership schools. I think there are principals like myself in these schools that are really working hard at challenging their own systems and putting some different stuff in place, but the issue will be whether our system believes in us enough and also believes enough or can fund the fact that these schools need to be resourced differently in order to put different systems in place.

While the sustainability of National Partnership funding is an important issue (and, indeed, the scheme has now ended), the allocation of resources to disadvantaged schools could be seen as an instance of the system actually 'believing' in these schools, even taking into account the restrictive and performative-based level of compliance that comes with it (as explained in the previous chapter). It is important to note how Carol uses phrases such as 'believes in us' and 'challenging their own systems'. This indicates a space Carol uses as principal to speak against government policy and bring specific issues to the agenda. This is very much an example of Foucault's (1981) idea of power as productive and working in an ascending manner. It is at the local level, that of the principal's practices, where power is exercised for the purposes Carol deems important and necessary. There is also the risk for Carol that the government may not 'believe in' principals enough to let them implement their own agendas based on their perceptions of need. It is in this space where tensions arise for school principals: that is, between the space provided by the National Partnership Agreements and compliance with the government in terms of meeting benchmarks, desktop audits and annual performance reviews.

One issue that has become paramount for Carol and Ridgeway is the presence at the school of a number of Polynesian refugees. In the following excerpt she talks about the challenges presented by these students in terms of required support:

> If we think about what EQ is doing for Polynesian support in our school, the kids have to pay to go to university, they have to pay upfront to go to TAFE, there's no support person from Education Queensland, there's no ESL support. Despite the fact . . . that they've been in New Zealand for two years and they've come from the islands, a lot of them can't speak English. But because they've come from New Zealand, they're not granted any ESL support. So, once again, we've got this situation where I'm having to find ESL funding and support to support these kids. Ninety per cent of them who sat NAPLAN are ESL in this school, you know. What support am I getting for those kids? Absolutely none. Unless they're new to Australia within two years, and coming via New Zealand is not new to Australia. So, yeah, we have to think outside the square as principals in these schools because it will be a long time before the Trans-Tasman Agreement is changed, which is a trade agreement.
>
> It's a really interesting situation. You know, there's no health support. They don't have Medicare cards. They don't have any access to education support. Fourteen out of my eighteen kids in year 12 are Polynesian who will get an OP 1 to 15, and not one of them will go

to university because they have to pay upfront. So what are we doing about that? We're doing nothing.

There are some really interesting challenges as a principal in this country at the moment because of a whole range of political decisions, and then they have some issues that they present for us as leaders.

This could be seen as an example of Carol exercising a form of 'fearless speech' (Foucault, 2001) in which she finds these students' situation 'intolerable' (Foucault, 1988) and thus constitutes herself as a political subject by seeking to improve their circumstances and opportunities. This could be considered outside of her traditional role as principal, but Carol feels the need to work towards a solution, enacting a form of advocacy on the students' behalf (Anderson, 2009). At the same time, her actions are more than just a form of advocacy. She is engaging in parrhesia. As we discussed in Chapter 3, this is linked to a particular social situation where the speaker and the audience have different statuses. That is, it involves risk for the speaker. Speaking critically about the education authorities at both state and federal levels certainly involves a level of risk for Carol. As stated earlier, as principal of a National Partnership school on a rolling short-term contract, her position is under constant scrutiny. Moreover, speaking out about what she feels are injustices has implications for the school, the rest of the staff, students and the broader community. By daring to speak out, Carol is undertaking a specific relationship with the self that designates an importance placed on speaking her truth rather than letting the status quo continue. She knows that perpetuating the status quo will result in a continued life of disadvantage for her students.

As a result, and in response to this issue, Carol has engaged with a range of different forms of elaboration or practices of ethical self-formation. For example:

> This year I've put Medicare forms, application forms, in all our enrolment packs . . . The issue of kids not having a Medicare form, a Medicare card, is disgusting and it's a problem here when they get hurt [because] I've got to pay the bloody medical bills. So, you know, there are some really practical things that I can do as a leader that people aren't really thinking about. So when they fill in all their application forms, they just pull the Medicare form out, I sign it as a witness, and I put it in an envelope and post it for them, and [soon] they've got a Medicare card.

Carol is quick to highlight that this practice of acting on students' behalf is not a form of deficit discourse because the students 'think they are not entitled to' a Medicare card, or do not know where to go to get one, or are unable to prove their identity. So, she recognises the difficulties for these students in understanding and accessing these types of resources.

Importantly, Carol's advocacy reflects acute awareness of how her students are silenced within the broader policy context – through (incorrect) assumptions that New Zealanders are all English speakers who thus do not require ESL support and through assumptions that these students and their families have knowledge of and understand how to access Australia's healthcare system. These are problems of political representation or misframing that call into question how mainstream frames conceptualise justice issues (Fraser, 2007). Carol recognises that such frames create boundaries around who and what count in relation to justice considerations. For her Polynesian students, these frames clearly exclude (Fraser, 2007; Keddie, 2012) and thus they compound their disadvantage in relation to ESL support and support for further education opportunities (see Sidhu and Taylor, 2007; Keddie, 2012).

In recognition of the fact that there is more to her ethical self-formation than simply advocating or truth-telling, Carol has also undertaken a range of particular forms of elaboration around her role and even beyond the traditional responsibilities of a typical school principal. These forms of elaboration include:

- increased liaising with her local government representative;
- choosing Political Science electives in Australian policy as parts of her Masters in Education;
- including Medicare forms in the enrolment packs for her Polynesian refugee students and helping them to fill them out correctly so that they can receive health benefits;
- taking up a position as an educational leadership/principal representative of the Queensland Teachers' Union;
- engaging with a number of Queensland universities in an attempt to set up scholarships for these students who are eligible to attend; and
- offering opportunities to gain fork-lift-driving qualifications to parents as well as students.

All of these points, or forms of elaboration, illuminate the necessity for Carol to find ways to be heard or make a difference beyond the context of Education Queensland in order to lead in socially just ways, especially given the disadvantages endured by Ridgeway's students and the local community. She explains her work as follows:

> I've become the principal's rep of the Queensland Teachers' Union. I've also scored a place as the educational leader on the Educational

Leadership Committee of the Queensland Teachers' Union . . . to work within a more political frame around raising some of the more complex issues and political issues that impact on schools and learning and teaching in our state . . . I've also joined the Education Sub-committee of the Australian Labour Party . . . [In] the Queensland branch there's a group of educationalists that advise the Prime Minister. I'm also part of that group . . . I try, you know, to raise the issues . . . that affect our everyday. And I'm actually enjoying working in that group, in that circle, because I'm working with like-minded people who understand it's not whingeing; it's understanding the complexities.

It is interesting to note that Carol distinguishes between speaking out or parrhesia and 'whingeing'. She is not whingeing but 'understanding the complexities' that are facing these communities and working out ways to overcome their disadvantages. Carol is making the most of the opportunities these positions present in order to speak out to those who have a say in determining the education and social policies that affect her students; and she knows that this is working in a more political frame as principal of Ridgeway. This is not to say that she does not devote much of her time to important matters of curriculum and pedagogy, but this mode of subjection requires her to recognise the needs of the students and community and then proceed to work on her leadership as ethical substance by working in a more political way as she feels this will result in better outcomes.

Leadership and counter-conduct

All of the practices detailed in the previous section are aspects of Carol's engagement with political discourse. They involve her responding to the specific needs of her context, which she claims the state education authority and federal government are not interested in addressing, given their prioritisation of quantitative data, accountability and managerialism. Commenting on her regular assessment, she explains:

So, my performance review is coming up. I won't mention these other issues because simply the system doesn't want to know. There are no excuses as the system is the party line, which, you know, I'm not. I've never made excuses and I'm not making excuses, and our data, as I said, is incredibly good and improving exponentially. It's not about making excuses. It's about understanding the complexity so that we can put processes in place to try to better our system . . . Yeah, it's interesting, and I guess that's a dilemma because really, you

know, it's a challenge for people . . . for leaders professionally,
I think, to not go there.

Carol makes a conscious effort not to mention all of the extra work she
does in terms of her political subjectivity as she says the education
department is not interested. In line with the prevalence of neoliberal
forms of reporting and accountability to high-stakes test scores, many of
Carol's activities are neither valued nor recognised as important parts of
her work. These practices entail Carol working at the local level, from
the ground up, rather than adhering to the top-down style of 'leadership'
that is promoted by the state education authorities and indeed by
much of the leadership literature and discourse. The initiatives she has
implemented correspond with Foucault's (1981) notion of an ascending
view of power: that is, from the grass roots up. Carol practises two main
forms of counter-conduct in this respect: first, as stated above, she engages
in parrhesia; and, second, she uses a form of active silence or silenced
discourse. The latter involves deliberately not mentioning certain
aspects of her work but also not referring to policies and other forms of
accountability with which she disagrees or that she feels do not help the
students and the local community.

Carol freely expresses her distaste for the intense compliance expectations around her role as she feels her time could be better spent in other
areas. For example, as well as the ongoing performance reviews and
desktop audits, she is expected to work within the *Leadership Matters*
framework[1] for her own professional development and the development
of other staff at Ridgeway. In another example of counter-conduct, she
explains why she doesn't find the standards document useful or a good
representation of her work:

CAROL: Other than providing the organisers and the framework for
  my professional development plan, I probably don't refer to the
  Leadership Matters document at all.
INTERVIEWER: Do you get some sense that there's an expectation that you
  will?
CAROL: We were given the *Leadership Matters* framework for our
  particular banding of principalship by the director general at
  the start of the year. To be honest with you, I haven't read it.
  I know the *Leadership Matters* framework inside out. I have read
  it many a time.[2] As you know, we've done some study around it,
  but I don't use it . . . If we really start to unravel and dig and
  think about and critique the *Leadership Matters* framework,
  it is actually quite removed from the day-to-day practice of a
  principal.

By openly confessing that she doesn't refer to *Learning Matters*, Carol is exercising a form of counter-conduct to the expectation by EQ that principals will work closely with the document. However, she also feels that the document is not an accurate or helpful depiction of principals' practice. Similar criticism of leadership standards documents has highlighted how standards are used to gain a sense of credibility for the field of educational leadership. Such criticism argues that these standards do not tend to be grounded in empirical research, are not reflective of actual practices in schools, and are often blind to alternative discourses (see, e.g., Anderson, 2001; English, 2006; Niesche, 2012, 2013). What is important in the above example is that Carol is exercising power by not referring to it. She employs this strategy in relation to the *MySchool* website, too:

> *MySchool* does not do this school community any favours; nor does it do this community any favours. In fact, it's quite degrading for them and, you know, this community over a long period of time tends to have a very negative attitude towards bureaucrats and this is just another example for them to say, 'Well, look at our government, they say they care but, you know, the performance of our kids is now out there for the world to see.' So, for me, the *MySchool* website – I don't mention it at all. I don't mention it in any of my documents. I don't talk about it with my staff or my parents. I don't refer parents to it. *MySchool* is not very helpful to me and this community, that's for sure.

These modes of subjection cannot adequately reflect or capture the context of Carol's school and the work of Ridgeway's teachers (see Ball, 2003). *MySchool*, in particular, washes out the 'big picture' contextual issues of poverty, violence and criminality that generate the injustices for Carol's students and position them within these measures as deficit and lacking (Fraser, 1997; Young, 1990). As we noted in Chapter 2, these indicators reflect de-contextualised and 'cold' knowledge (see Glatter, 2012).

In addition to the silence around the *Leadership Matters* framework, Carol uses silence as a form of counter-conduct to this technique of governmentality. By not speaking about it, Carol is attempting to resist the influence of the school's poor performance data. This constitutes a form of silenced discourse as a conscious strategy, or, as Lyotard (1988) says, 'silence is a phrase'. Carol thus tries to insert counter-narratives about the action she is taking in relation to the 'bigger issues' that are affecting her students, and also about the caring emotional support that the school provides for those students. It is through the tensions between these two roles that her subjectivity shifts. On the one hand, she has appointed a director of student achievement, who is actively working to report her quantitative performance data to the government as a form of compliance. On the other hand, she actively avoids discussing the *MySchool* website and the *Leadership Matters* framework in a form of silenced discourse.

Carol is very candid about the challenges she faces, and acknowledges that she still has issues to address. For instance:

> There's some stuff that I do that isn't very socially just and I know that and I don't know how to manage it. Suspending kids for smoking, you know. For three weeks after the holidays, our kids don't come back to school. You know, fifty kids can't come back to school because they can't give up the smokes. When they do come back and they have a smoke, I suspend them. So, there's that real philosophical argy-bargy that happens inside you constantly about good order and management, social good, keeping a safe environment, honouring the law of the land around smoking in government buildings, around smoking and their age, around the fact that these kids are in my care, and their parents are probably not expecting me to allow them to smoke. So, there's that real argy-bargy that happens philosophically around what do I do? We've tried the Quit programme; the kids don't stick at it. We've tried the Online programme; the kids don't stick at it. They don't want to give up smoking. Smoking is a stress release. They will tell you it's better than cutting [their] arms ... And we suspend. So, there's some stuff I don't do well and I don't have the answers for that.

Most educators will be able to relate to Carol's internal anguish over these issues. Her comments vividly illustrate the emotional and sometimes physical toll that working in such schools and communities can exert on a teacher or principal. Carol talks of the 'philosophical argy-bargy' around making these decisions that can sometimes go against the social justice principles she is trying to uphold. She clearly understands that it is her responsibility to suspend students for smoking, yet she also acknowledges that smoking relieves stress for some of them, which may prevent them from indulging in more violent forms of self-harm. Many principals face similar ethical dilemmas in their day-to-day leadership work.

Conclusion

In this chapter we have identified a range of forms of elaboration and modes of subjection for Carol as she engages with her telos of social justice. Important to this ideal are practices of engaging with political issues beyond the school gates. This involves engaging with a wide body of constituents and taking up positions and roles in other organisations. Other practices are supporting students' needs, such as helping them to fill out Medicare forms, as well as the important practices of speaking out, or parrhesia, and even counter-conduct and active silence on some issues, such as the *MySchool* website. Foucault's notion of counter-conduct is useful here, not as a concept of resistance *against* forms of domination, but rather as a way of working in the spaces of freedom of the accountability logic as a part of governmentality and disciplinary practices. The examples of Carol's leadership in this low SES community 'make sense' only when analysed in this context and not on the basis of importing or applying de-contextualised models of leadership.

This case study illuminates the tensions for the school principal in meeting the demands of new accountabilities at the same time as working for equity and social justice for disadvantaged groups. Analysis of these tensions allows the different subject positions of the school principal to be brought to light. It is then possible to see how power is exercised at this level on the principal, through the principal, and by the principal, constituting her as a particular subject in the specificity of the school context. Carol has had to weigh meeting Education Queensland's requirements against meeting the needs of her students in terms of the impact of social context on those students and the school. The spaces within these discourses allow Carol to exercise a form of counter-conduct and work in the form of intervention and advocacy for her students, thus she is constituted as a political subject; a subject position that is rare among the more typical and popular approaches to educational leadership. Carol is not simply implementing the models espoused by such capabilities documents as *Leadership Matters*; rather, she is engaging with the needs of the community that sometimes may sit at odds with the directions and expectations of the education department. Of course, there is a high price to pay for the principal if she fails to meet performance expectations in terms of literacy and numeracy results as well as her own performance review, but these are factors she must consider when taking action. It is clear that Carol believes the price being paid by her students as a result of a system that has continually let them down is much higher, and needs to be addressed immediately. While it is not our intention to offer this case study as an exemplar of 'good leadership', it is certainly an example of leadership in action, as it happens.

In Chapters 6 and 7 we move to the next case study: the Clementine-led alliance in England. This provides more examples of leadership practices that are working towards ideals of social justice.

Notes

1 This is the state education authority's leadership standards document, although recently it has moved away from the term 'standards' and now prefers the term 'capabilities'. See Niesche (2011, 2012) for a critique of this document.
2 At first sight, this would seem to contradict Carol's comment that she has not read *Leadership Matters*. However, we assume that her earlier comment refers specifically to the fact that she does not consult the document for the purposes of her performance review.

References

Anderson, G. (2001). Disciplining leaders: A critical discourse analysis of the ISLLC National Examination and Performance Standards in educational administration. *International Journal of Leadership in Education*, 4 (3), 199–216.

Anderson, G. (2009). *Advocacy leadership: Toward a post-reform agenda in education*. London and New York, Routledge.

Ball, S. (2003). The teacher's soul and the terrors of performativity. *Journal of Education Policy*, 18 (2), 215–228.

Dardot, P. and Laval, C. (2013). *The new way of the world: On neoliberal society*. London, Verso.

Deleuze, G. (1992). Postscript on the societies of control. *October*, 59, 3–7.

English, F. W. (2006). The unintended consequences of a standardized knowledge base in advancing educational leadership preparation. *Educational Administration Quarterly*, 42 (3), 461–472.

Foucault, M. (1977). *Discipline and punish*. New York, Pantheon Books.

Foucault, M. (1981). *The history of sexuality*, Volume I. London, Penguin.

Foucault, M. (1988). *Politics, philosophy, culture: Interviews and other writings, 1977–1984*. Edited by L. Kritzman. New York, Routledge.

Foucault, M. (1991). Governmentality. In G. Burchill, C. Gordon and P. Miller (eds) *The Foucault effect: Studies in governmentality*. Chicago, University of Chicago Press.

Foucault, M. (2001). *Fearless speech*. Edited by J. Pearson. Los Angeles, CA, Semiotext(e).

Foucault, M. (2002). The subject and power. In J. D. Faubion (ed.) *Essential works of Foucault, 1954–1984*, Volume I: *Power*. London, Penguin.

Foucault, M. (2007). *Security, territory, population: Lectures at the College de France 1977–1978*. New York, Picador.

Fraser, N. (1997). *Justice interruptus: Critical reflections on the 'postsocialist' condition*. New York, Routledge.

Fraser, N. (2007). Feminist politics in the age of recognition: A two-dimensional approach to gender justice. *Studies in Social Justice*, 1 (1), 23–35.

Fullan, M. (1993). *Change forces*. New York, Falmer Press.

Glatter, R. (2012). Persistent preoccupations: The rise and rise of school autonomy and accountability in England. *Educational Management Administration and Leadership*, 40 (5), 559–575.

Keddie, A. (2012). *Educating for diversity and social justice*. New York, Routledge.

Lingard, R. (2012). Policy as numbers: Ac/counting for educational research. *Australian Educational Researcher*, 38 (4), 355–382.

Lingard, R. and Sellar, S. (2013). 'Catalyst data': Perverse systemic effects of audit and accountability in Australian schooling. *Journal of Education Policy*, 28 (5), 634–656.

Lyotard, J. F. (1988). *The differend: Phrases in dispute*. Minneapolis, University of Minnesota Press.

Niesche, R. (2011). *Foucault and educational leadership: Disciplining the principal*. London, Routledge.

Niesche, R. (2012). Politicising articulation: Applying Lyotard's work to the use of standards in educational leadership. *International Journal of Leadership in Education*, 16 (2), 220–233.

Niesche, R. (2013). *Deconstructing educational leadership: Derrida and Lyotard*. London, Routledge.

Rose, N. (1990). *Powers of freedom: Reframing political thought*. Cambridge, Cambridge University Press.

Sarra, C. (2003). *Cherbourg State School, strong and smart, What Works program: Improving outcomes for Indigenous students*. From www.whatworks.edu.au/dbAction.do?cmd=displaySitePage1andsubcmd=selectandid=111, accessed 11 March 2015.

Sidhu, R. and Taylor, S. (2007). Education provision for refugee youth: Left to chance. *Journal of Sociology*, 43 (3), 283–300.

Young, I. M. (1990). *Justice and the politics of difference*. Princeton, NJ, Princeton University Press.

6   The Clementine-led alliance

Articulating a telos of social justice

In a sense we all have a mission statement, which is to prepare our students for the next stage in their lives, but for us that is recognising that in London, to get a job, to be a worthy and productive member of society, to have an identity, to have choices involves success in exams. It's not empty, it's very real . . . especially for us, given the state of the British economy . . . So, you know, in terms of morality, one of the things that we're most proud of from last year is that . . . every single one of [our sixteen-year-olds] is in [education], productive employment or training. And that's an achievement. And it's an Ofsted measure. And it's not a bad measure.

(Ms J)

These comments are from Ms J, the head teacher at the Clementine Academy, the lead school within an alliance of schools in one of the most diverse boroughs of outer London. As detailed in Chapter 2, the schools came together as part of a broader government initiative, the National Teaching Schools programme. Clementine was selected as one of the first hundred schools to participate in this programme (in 2011) on the basis of its outstanding performance in the areas of student achievement and school leadership. The alliance comprises of approximately twenty secondary and primary schools (of various types and models).

We begin this chapter with the same quote from Ms J that opened the book because it provides a sense of the alliance's 'mission': that is, to 'prepare students for the next stage in their lives . . . to get a job, to be worthy and productive members of society'. This mission of supporting all students to achieve educational success was embraced by all of the schools in the group. Effective networking within the group was seen to be significant in supporting this mission and there were specific leadership practices that fostered such networking. The group seemed to work well together because each school's autonomy was respected and there were commonly agreed structures for encouraging collaboration. The workings of this leadership telos and its relationship to the social justice pursuit of learner improvement are explored in this chapter.

Before embarking on these analyses, we introduce the Clementine-led alliance and provide important details about the matters of context shaping the data and arguments presented. Key here is the description of the schools in the alliance and an explication of the research processes from which the data arose. We also revisit some of the information presented in Chapter 2 about the English policy context within, and against, which this alliance operates. As with the previous two chapters, we explore the ethical dimensions of leadership by drawing on Foucault's work, but our focus in this and the following chapter is on one school's leadership and relationship with a number of allied schools, rather than the leadership of a single school.

In this chapter we provide an account of Clementine's ethical group leadership in relation to its prioritising of school autonomy, school collaboration and learner improvement. This form of relationship between schools provides a nice counterbalance to the previous two chapters, which were focused on one school and its principal. We examine this leadership in relation to the broader moral codes or modes of subjection mandated by the Department for Education. We highlight the productive role and effects of these modes in relation to the group's telos of leadership and social justice.

In Chapter 7 we explore practices of advocacy, truth-telling and counter-conduct within the Clementine-led alliance. We consider the significance and necessity of these practices in Clementine leading ethically amid the segregation and inequities created by autonomous education systems and the demands and high stakes of the audit culture. We highlight how such advocacy and counter-conduct are integral to the socially just leadership practices at Clementine, especially in relation to supporting 'vulnerable' member schools. We also, however, examine some of the tensions associated with Clementine's leadership. These are evident, in particular, in the practices of counter-conduct *within* the alliance when member schools challenge some aspects of Clementine's leadership in order to protect their autonomy.

Portrait of the Clementine-led alliance

One of the most interesting aspects of the Clementine-led alliance is the diversity of schools in the group. There are twelve secondary schools and eight primary schools, ranging in model and type. Many of the secondary schools are academies, while most of the primary schools are maintained local authority schools. The schools also cover an array of different specialisations, from technical schools, sports-, science- or arts-focused academies to single-sex schools and schools for students with learning difficulties. According to Ofsted (Office for Standards in Education) standards, the schools also vary in 'quality', with gradings ranging from 'outstanding', to 'good', to 'requires improvement' (none of the schools are graded 'inadequate'). There is, however, a key similarity across all of the schools as all of them cater to very high levels of minority diversity. The cultural, ethnic and faith diversity of students reflects the demographics of the borough within which many of the schools are situated. In this borough, which is one of the largest in Greater London, 150 languages are spoken and all of the major world religions are represented. Parts of the borough are economically deprived while others are not. This diversity reflects immigration patterns arising from the borough's close proximity to a busy international airport, with new arrivals to the country settling and shifting largely in response to employment opportunities and changes in socio-economic status.

The seven schools that feature in this chapter reflect the broader diversity of schools within the alliance. The tone of each school leader seemed to generate a sense of each school's climate and ethos. The sense of poise and strong confidence radiating from Ms J's friendly and efficacious manner, for example, well encapsulates the climate at the lead school, Clementine. This large and well-resourced academy, with expansive grounds and friendly learning huts and resource centres, clearly lives its outstanding status and renown in the education community. While the tenor is welcoming and energetic, there is also a seriousness and high degree of application in how the students behave.

Similar seriousness and application are evident in Mr G's school – a large, non-academised technical college that proudly and loudly displays its recent Ofsted grade of 'outstanding' in enormous banners in the expansive school foyer and at various other locations around the site. Indeed, following our interview, Mr G, whose pride and confidence in relation to the value of his school were palpable, offered several gifts: a key ring, button and sticker all emblazoned with the words 'We are outstanding!' Attaining this status was a significant achievement, given the school's history as a disadvantaged and underperforming establishment. After major refurbishments, it now exudes a sense of corporate-ordered efficiency.

This climate contrasted markedly with Mr R's school, where the grounds and buildings seem a little tired and unkempt. This large academy with many disadvantaged students and a larger than average number in receipt of free school meals (a proxy indicator of class disadvantage as this programme generally caters to children whose parents receive social welfare support) is rated 'good' by Ofsted. Mr R spoke in quiet and measured tones about the struggles his school faced in the current climate and his determined commitment to supporting his students through these struggles.

Ms M exuded a similar sense of quiet determination about the challenges facing her school, a large secondary academy for girls that is also rated 'good' by Ofsted. Sandwiched geographically between two 'outstanding' all-girls private schools, Ms M's concerns were with the unfairness of comparative judgements across the three schools given the greater disadvantages confronting her less privileged student cohort. In contrast with Mr R's school, however, the climate at Ms M's is bustling and bright. The school's studious tone is captured in a large professional banner in the small, homely foyer, which depicts several girls in lab coats and protective eye-wear, earnestly engaged in a science experiment.

Ms E's small primary school is similarly bustling and bright, even though the buildings and grounds appear, like Mr R's school, a little tired and unkempt. This school is not well resourced and, indeed, is struggling financially to manage its facilities and programmes. Despite these struggles, it is warm and welcoming, reflecting Ms E's generous and open manner. She projected a strong sense of pride but also protectiveness of her 'not so popular' school and 'quirky' students. Notwithstanding the high levels of demand associated with economic disadvantage and English as an Additional Language (EAL) requirements, the school's most recent Ofsted grade was a respectable 'good'.

Mr T's large secondary academy is also considered 'good' by Ofsted. Like Mr R's academy, at Mr T's there is a larger than average proportion of students in receipt of free school meals. The cement-rendered buildings and grounds are huge and stark, with expanses of concreted 'play' areas surrounded by the large and forbidding iron security fence that defines the school's perimeter. Mr T's concerns, as a relatively new head teacher at this school, were with stimulating a more proactive and innovative ethos and approach. His tone projected a sense of pragmatism about what was required to achieve this ideal, but also high levels of motivation about what is possible.

The final of the schools featured in this chapter is Mr I's secondary school, the only sponsored academy out of the seven (all of the other academies are converter academies). As explained in Chapter 2, most academies choose to become autonomous, and these converter academies are generally 'outstanding' or high-performing schools. Sponsored academies, on the other hand, are generally underperforming schools that are placed under the direction of an institution or group of institutions that is then held accountable for improving their performance (DfE, 2013). Mr I's school is sponsored by a stockbroker, a university and two multinational businesses. For Mr I, the school's Ofsted rating of 'requiring improvement' reflects, to a great extent, the high levels of

Table 6.1 Schools in the Clementine-led alliance

Head teacher	School type	Ofsted rating[1]
Ms J	Lead school: 'Clementine' Secondary converter academy	Outstanding
Mr G	Secondary maintained technical school	Outstanding
Mr R	Secondary converter academy	Good
Ms M	Secondary converter all-girls academy	Good
Ms E	Primary maintained school	Good
Mr T	Secondary converter academy	Good
Mr I	Secondary sponsored academy	Requiring improvement

social deprivation within the school and its local community. The student cohort is by far the most disadvantaged of the seven schools, with nearly half of the students in receipt of free school meals (nearly double the national average) and a high proportion requiring special education services.

Table 6.1 provides an overview of the seven schools presented in this chapter.

Locating the research

As noted in Chapter 1, the case studies featured in this book derive from two discrete research projects. While these projects share a similar agenda in relation to both their focus on social justice and leadership and their research design, the data presented reflect different journeys and processes that will be detailed here (as they were in Chapter 4 for the Ridgeway case study) to provide a context for understanding the data.

In this chapter, data are drawn from a broader study of the Clementine Academy aimed at exploring 'productive' structures and practices for addressing issues of equity and student diversity. Clementine was selected on the basis of its strong reputation in this respect. It has been an academy for several years and has consistently received an 'outstanding' Ofsted rating. It is well recognised in the education community as forward thinking and innovative, and has, according to Ofsted, 'excelled against the odds'. The focus on the alliance and on the National Teaching Schools programme was prompted through discussions with Clementine's leadership staff. This initiative seemed to be a particularly significant avenue in relation to the school's efforts to spread productive and just schooling practices.

As briefly outlined in Chapter 2, the National Teaching Schools initiative is a wide-ranging programme supported by England's Department for Education and the National College for Teaching and Leadership. It is focused on school improvement through teacher and leadership professional learning and development. This focus is fostered through a key aim of the initiative – to generate productive partnerships and alliances between schools. At the time of writing there were around 360 teaching schools, and the government was planning to expand this number to 500 by 2015. A teaching school is invariably an 'outstanding' school, as evidenced by high levels of student performance and head teacher leadership, and a strong track record of working collaboratively with other schools. One or more teaching schools are responsible for leading an alliance of schools that commit to working together with the support of this leadership. These schools often represent a diverse range of school types, as is illustrated by the Clementine-led alliance. Membership of an alliance is voluntary, with the ties to its agenda and practices flexible (Hargreaves, 2011).

Teaching schools are being touted by the Department for Education as the 'real champions of school-to-school improvement and collaboration' in drawing 'together the very best that schools in their alliance have to offer and ensuring that more children in more schools experience the benefits of great teaching and leadership as a result' (National College for School Leadership, 2011: 4). The idea here is that such improvement will be self-sustaining because the initiative is school-led and -based, with responsibility for assuring high-quality work generated through the alliance itself. The imperative for teaching schools to be enterprising also aligns with this notion of self-sustainment. While they are funded over three years (a total of £150,000), this funding decreases each year, with the expectation that they will ultimately generate their own income to self-fund their alliance programmes.

As noted in Chapter 2, teaching schools are a significant cog in the coalition government's 'Big Society' machinery, which is designed to transform the English school system from local democratic governance to devolved private management. They have therefore generated considerable concern because of their potential to contribute to rearticulations of what constitutes quality teachers and teaching along narrow, uncritical and prescriptive lines, and because of their role in transferring control for teacher training from universities to schools.

We acknowledge the ideological and practical limitations of this initiative – limitations we neither condone nor support. Rather, in this and the next chapter, with the help of Foucault's theoretical tools, we attempt to highlight how Clementine has worked within this initiative to support other schools in the alliance. We thus focus specifically on the processes of collaboration between schools supported by the National Teaching Schools programme. We do contend, as we mentioned in Chapter 2 and consistent with Hill's research (Hill, 2010; Hill et al., 2012), that teaching schools, while far from unproblematic, are likely preferable to other structural reforms instated by the Department for Education, such as academy chains.

The fieldwork for this study was conducted over two months in the first half of 2013. It primarily involved in-depth interviews with a number of key staff (who were responsible for equity) and students, but also included observations of classroom and school practice/behaviour. The data presented in this chapter were gathered from individual interviews with the head teachers of the seven alliance schools described earlier. Several interviews of approximately one hour's duration were conducted with the head teacher (Ms J), her assistant (Ms C) and the project manager (Ms S) at Clementine over the course of the fieldwork. In these interviews, as mentioned earlier, the significance of the National Teaching Schools programme became apparent, and this provided the impetus for the arrangement of interviews with other alliance members. The head teachers of all twenty alliance schools were subsequently contacted via email to invite them to participate. The resulting interviews (generally an hour in duration) were conducted with all of those who responded positively to this email and made themselves available (introduced earlier as Mr G, Mr R, Ms M, Ms E, Mr T and Mr I). Most of these head teachers were highly experienced in their roles, and all of their schools had been members of the alliance for at least one year.

Interviews with these participants sought to explore the potential of the alliance through the National Teaching Schools initiative to improve school performance. Questions were loosely structured and prompted participants to comment and elaborate on their experiences of being members of the alliance. The focus was on exploring members' thoughts about:

* issues of leading and leadership;
* what had been most and least productive for their schools in terms of improving practice;
* relationships, collaborations and the sharing of expertise and ideas; and
* key future challenges facing the alliance.

The analysis of data presented in this chapter draws on Foucault's fourfold ethical framework. The first level of analysis articulates the telos of leadership within the Clementine-led alliance: that is, a form of leadership that prioritises individual school autonomy and school collaboration as goals. We locate this telos within the broader parameters of Clementine's role as a teaching school as part of the National Teaching Schools initiative. The moral codes of this and other departmentally sanctioned initiatives were analysed in relation to how they shaped/ impacted on the group's leadership telos.

The second level of analysis articulates the telos of social justice informing the alliance: that of improving the learning outcomes of all students. Our analysis in this section also locates this telos within the broader moral codes or modes of subjection mandated by the Department for Education and, in particular, those associated with external measures of accountability in the form of exam results and Ofsted evaluations. Again, our focus was to examine how such codes shaped and impacted on the group's telos of social justice.

A telos of leadership

As we discussed in relation to Carol's principalship at Ridgeway in Chapter 3, leadership is a moral and ethical activity where, in Foucauldian terms, 'moral' refers to a set of prescribed norms or values, and 'ethics' refers to the behaviours or conduct of individuals in relation to these moral norms (Foucault, 1992). With regard to the Clementine-led alliance, the parameters of the National Teaching Schools initiative might be viewed as the norms of morality within which Clementine, as a school, conducts itself as the leader of the other schools. As with Carol's leadership, at Clementine this conduct was not fixed but fluid and shifted according to various demands and interrelations. However, Clementine prioritised certain ways of working as key to leading an effective network. These ways of working were explained by Ms J:

> [With] some teaching schools, it's like 'We're the teaching school, we're the experts.' We have never really worked in that way because I think pride and falls come together; because I think that way you miss out on opportunities to develop the best of what's happening ... What we haven't done is say, 'This is what's happening at Clementine, take it on, it will solve all your problems.' We've never been driven by that. I mean, I think the teaching school movement is not driven by that.
>
> (Ms J)

This is a telos that rejects an 'expert' or authoritarian model of leadership. Such rejection is an example of this school's ethical substance – an awareness that the power relations between Clementine and the other schools may lead to domination or an abuse of authority. It is not a fixed subject position but a way of working that is relational and responsive to particular social circumstances or modes of subjection. This form of ethical substance, of a particular type of leadership to be exercised, requires ongoing work to achieve the particular telos in terms of its relations with the other schools in the alliance. As with Carol's leadership, this ethical substance is intimately linked to the modes of subjection mandated by the state (in this case the authority granted to Clementine under the National Teaching Schools initiative). Ms J recognises that such modes are powerful in shaping behaviour and actions both to open up and to close down 'opportunities' within the alliance. For Ms J, her ethical way of leading as a teaching school means not being 'driven by' an 'expert' approach because she sees this as 'miss[ing] out on opportunities to develop the best of what's happening'. The modes of subjection of the National Teaching Schools initiative are, for Ms J, a positive force in this respect in their promotion of schools working together collaboratively.

This 'open' and 'genuine' approach' to schools 'helping each other' was endorsed by other head teachers in the alliance, as Mr T remarked:

> The idea of schools helping schools is the way to go for me. If you have got an open approach and you are willing, genuinely, to work with other schools in order to make them better, as well as to make your own school better, that's always going to be better than waiting for someone else to come and provide that service for you.
>
> (Mr T)

Consistent with this approach, Ms J, as alliance leader, highlighted the significance of supporting individual school autonomy. Indeed, she noted that such autonomy was instrumental in members agreeing to, and adopting, a positive attitude towards working with them. This positivity was clear in how members described their schools' roles in the alliance. Mr G, Mr I and Mr R, for example, described their schools as enjoying their position of autonomy within the group, especially in terms of feeling free to take up, modify or reject particular interventions or strategies on offer but also to contribute their skills and expertise to the group. Mr R's comments were illustrative of this view:

> It feels like we're part of a network more than we're being led in a network. So . . . I suppose I take from that what I feel is right for the school and I try and give back because I want to give as well as take . . . I don't kind of feel that I'm particularly led . . . This is a network of which we are a contributor . . . I mean I think that any other model would just ... no head teacher of a school is going to be told what to do by another head teacher, in a sense, and they haven't tried to do that at all, I think, and they would agree with that. So, it's very much 'These are the opportunities and how do we work together to develop stuff?'
>
> (Mr R)

These comments reflect the autonomy and control that are important in fostering effective networking between schools in terms of voluntary membership and flexible ties (see Muijs et al., 2011; Black-Hawkins, 2007; Hargreaves, 2011; Chapman et al., 2005). In Mr R's view, the leadership within the alliance is not 'expert' led but rather inclusive and open. It seems that the member schools do not feel controlled or obliged to take up particular practices, but rather 'take from' the alliance in terms of 'what feels right' for their own school contexts while also feeling valued as contributors and supported to 'work together to develop stuff'. Foucault (2000) makes the point that ethics is linked to forms of freedom to act and not simply in response to harsh, punitive mechanisms. Therefore, there are spaces within the alliance for schools to act, and to undertake particular sets of practices that are required for their own teloi and approaches to leadership. This is also an example of the productive aspect to power (Foucault, 1981). This type of freedom or way of leading was juxtaposed against the perceived loss of autonomy and independence involved in being a member of a chain, as Mr R explained:

> It's not like signing up to [Big Chain X] or [Big Chain Y] or something. This is a very, very different kind of relationship and it's a much more, you know, a collaborative partnership arrangement, and we wouldn't dream of being part of anything that wasn't like that, really.
> (Mr R)

In light of the tendency for some chains to undermine school autonomy and independence, and be unresponsive to local/context specificity (see Glatter, 2012), these remarks position Clementine's approach in significant contrast. Along these lines, Ms E described Clementine's leadership as a 'people' approach to school improvement that is 'robust' but not 'punitive'. She compared this with what can 'happen externally': for example, when Ofsted assessments are used to 'punish' and 'whip' teachers 'into shape'. Consistent with Mr R's remarks, Ms E similarly viewed Clementine's approach to school improvement as mindful of, and responsive to, context. As she stated, it is always 'about the school and the people in it' (see Muijs et al., 2011).

Autonomy and collaboration, then, were key priorities in Clementine's leadership telos, and there were multiple processes through which such priorities were supported and negotiated. Key here were efforts to share skills and knowledge throughout the alliance (Muijs et al., 2011; Black-Hawkins, 2007). For the project manager at Clementine, Ms S, this was about 'cascading high-impact practice around and between schools'. There was strong recognition of the existence of such expertise and its positive impacts on building capacity within the alliance. For example, most of the head teachers spoke positively about their access to different professional development opportunities and resources as members of the alliance. As Mr T commented, being a member of the alliance meant that he had 'access to some outstanding practices' and could 'dialogue' with 'fantastic heads'. Other members, including Mr R (in his earlier remarks in this section), emphasised the significance of their school contributing to the alliance. For example, Mr I stated, 'We also seek to contribute as well because we've got some really good individuals here and I believe by contributing you can have an impact on other schools'.

Clementine was actively committed to supporting such contributions – in Ms J's words, to 'bringing out and recognising the expertise of particular schools and empowering them to lead'. She explained that this was about 'solving problems' that all the schools were dealing with, but it was also about 'building on understandings of what works where'. Ms S referred here to Clementine's focus on supporting 'talent to bubble up' within the alliance, as she stated, 'we have so much talent in our schools'. Her view, like Ms J's, was that the school needed to assist other schools in the alliance to develop quality and sustainable programmes that could be shared and that they could lead. She described this as 'freeing up the capacity in those schools'.

Sharing expertise and fostering collaboration across the group were strategic endeavours. As Ms J remarked, 'just [being] well meaning and wanting to help students is fluffy and it doesn't work. It has to be more strategic than that.' A crucial aspect of developing and spreading productive practice within the alliance was through common programmes that the group agreed were of particular quality in their facilitation of school improvement (Muijs et al., 2011; Earl and Katz, 2005). As with Clementine's rejection of an authoritarian model of leadership, this way of leading is another example of ethical substance that reflected and responded to particular modes of subjection. In this case, the modes of subjection for sharing expertise and collaboration within the alliance were in the form of accredited and nationally recognised programmes aimed explicitly at improving the quality of teaching, learning and leading across the group. Many of the head teachers spoke in positive terms about how particular programmes – for example, the Outstanding Teacher Programme (OTP), developed by the company Olevi and accredited by the National College for School Leadership – were useful mechanisms in this respect. Drawing on the expertise and leadership of outstanding teachers at Clementine, this professional development initiative supports other teachers in the alliance to improve their practice through face-to-face sessions and classroom observations that foster a critical analysis of classroom pedagogy. This programme was seen as important in building capacity within schools, as Mr G and Ms E explained:

> The thing that has probably had the biggest impact on us is the Outstanding Teacher Programme. I'm getting three people trained as facilitators to lead it and disseminate here . . . My teachers can take part and they love it [because] they get to work with good teachers in other schools.
>
> (Mr G)

> What they've offered us, and we've taken it up wholeheartedly, is the opportunity for myself and a colleague to train as facilitators in the . . . OTP programme; to train up other colleagues in other schools but also to use some of that wealth of knowledge with our own colleagues here . . . This gives us a much sharper view of . . . what we are doing, what [the] quality [of our] teaching is like.
>
> (Ms E)

In further reference to providing a clearer view of quality teaching and what it might look like, Mr R referred to the OTP as 'putting' 'outstanding' teaching 'on the map' for his school and increasing aspirations for staff:

> The OTP, I think, has been really good. One of the things we wanted to do was to increase our percentage of outstanding teaching and it's kind of put it on the map a bit for us, because before then we were a bit . . . reticent about 'outstanding', using the word 'outstanding'. You know, do we want to be all sort of 'outstanding'? And actually it's kind of helped create a bit of a culture shift to say, 'Actually, no, we *should* aspire to be "outstanding", and let's use that language.' It has had a big impact, both for those people and for others in setting the bar higher and increasing aspirations for staff.
>
> (Mr R)

Another programme that members identified as helping them to articulate their expertise and develop a common language of quality practice was the Challenge the Gap programme. This programme is supported by the Education Endowment Foundation, and is designed to narrow the gap between free school meal pupils and their peers. Challenge the Gap, like the OTP, provided a common frame that fostered the sharing of ideas and mutual reflection to, in Ms S's words, identify 'the interventions and strategies that have the highest impact [in] narrowing this gap'. Mr I regarded his school's involvement in this programme as a positive move, especially given the high levels of social deprivation within his student cohort. In his view, the programme supported a greater focus on these students and improved their learning outcomes through shared understandings about the best teaching.

For Ms J, the 'advantage of [these programmes lay in] bringing people from different schools within the alliance together. So, at a classroom teacher level, we're getting working relationships and social relationships.' Clementine also encouraged 'different people from different schools to lead these programmes' in contexts other than their own. Moreover, it was always the case that Clementine staff led professional learning in other schools rather than at Clementine in order, in Ms J's words, to 'give them distance to be evaluative about what's happening here'. The purpose of this, according to Ms J, was to promote an understanding of the nature and context of the different schools in the alliance. The collaboration embedded in programmes like OTP certainly supports interdependence in ways that bind members of a network together and make cooperative action possible (Muijs et al., 2011). Under these arrangements, schools are compelled to work together and within their own structures to improve their practice.

These forms of ethical substance – namely, respecting individual school autonomy and employing a strategic approach to facilitating collaboration – reflect key elements of effective networking (Muijs et al., 2011; Black-Hawkins, 2007; Lieberman and McLaughlin, 1992). They also, importantly, reflect a sense of equitable distribution (see Fraser, 2009) in terms of all schools being able to 'give and take' from the alliance, depending on their needs. The equitable distribution of skills and expertise was a primary emphasis for Clementine in its relations with the other schools. As Ms S explained:

> If we were successful then all the schools in the alliance would be offering something for the benefit of everyone else. Not everyone would take up everything but . . . in a perfect alliance, every school would be offering something into the mix, as well as taking from the alliance.
>
> (Ms S)

Importantly, however, and consistent with the comments made by Mr R and Mr I that were quoted above, there were differentiated expectations in relation to each member school's capacities to contribute to the alliance. As will become more evident in the next chapter, there was a recognition that less privileged schools in the alliance were not as able to contribute to the group as the more privileged schools, and, indeed, required greater support from the alliance (Fraser, 1997).

Notwithstanding this, there was a sense that all schools could make a contribution to the alliance in some way. For some schools, according to Ms J, instilling recognition of their capacities to contribute was an important step, as she explained with reference to a particular head teacher during a recent leadership workshop:

[She] said, 'I've always regarded my school as the bottom of the pile.' What I have learned from this [alliance] is that we're not at the bottom of the pile, and although a school may seem to be the least successful, there is an awful lot that more allegedly successful schools can learn from us.

(Ms J)

The remarks we have quoted thus far reveal that Clementine's focus on autonomy and collaboration is highly valued by the alliance members. It seems that most members feel that they are accorded a voice in decision-making about their role in the alliance and freedom and flexibility in how they view and take up opportunities within the alliance (Fraser, 1997). The focus on autonomy within commonly agreed structures for encouraging collaboration and school improvement seems to create the democratic conditions that are required by all schools in the alliance if they are to participate actively. Schools that may feel marginalised or at the 'bottom of the pile' (as the comments above suggest), or in need of support to be more aspirational (like at Mr R's school), can contribute in the same way as more 'allegedly successful' schools. They are also free to accept or reject particular interventions in line with what they see as appropriate for their schools. Hence, there is space for 'give as well as take' (to use Mr R's words). Imperative here is Clementine's rejection of an expert model of leadership in favour of finding 'opportunities [across the alliance] to develop the best of what's happening' (Ms J).

As with Carol's leadership at Ridgeway, Clementine's leadership of the alliance is a dynamic and complex process that is ethically driven and contextually responsive. Pursuing a telos of leadership that priori- tises autonomy and collaboration for Clementine is an ongoing process of negotiation and reflection. It is a process of becoming rather than a fixed state of working (Foucault, 2000). As with Carol's approach to leadership, Clementine's ways of working are constructed, recon- structed and negotiated in light of the contextual priorities and demands of the alliance. Thus, the telos of leadership is constantly evolving, predominantly, as we saw in the preceding section, within the moral codes or modes of subjection that have been mandated or sanctioned by the Department for Education. Within such codes as the National Teaching Schools initiative and the OTP, Clementine is granted a sub- stantial level of authority over the other schools in the alliance. Rather than using this authority in oppressive ways, however, Clementine works within these codes to support rather than undermine individual school autonomy and collaboration. Ms J's school does not draw on these codes in authoritarian or punitive ways but rather in supportive and productive ways.

A key aspect of the ethical work undertaken by those at Clementine is to remain constantly aware of the potential for misuse of power – to manage the space of power that exists in the relationships and to manage it in a non-authoritarian manner (Foucault, 2000). These issues are at the heart of what Foucault refers to as 'care of the self'. Clementine exercises practices of care of the self – that is, it looks after its own affairs – but it also conducts itself ethically in relation to the other schools in the alliance. In this regard, care of the self is relational to the well-being of others (Foucault, 2000). As a result, this telos of leadership becomes more possible with the alliance schools conferring with, and adopting, the processes of autonomy and collaboration that Clementine promotes. We explore this telos further in relation to its focus on improving student achievement in the next section.

A telos of social justice

Like Carol's view of social justice at Ridgeway, supporting students to achieve regardless of their background circumstances was a strong concern within the Clementine-led alliance. Supporting improved learning outcomes for all students within and beyond the alliance was, according to Ms J, a 'moral imperative'. Other members of the alliance shared a similar commitment to this imperative. Mr R, for example, who described Clementine as a 'very values-driven organisation', spoke of his school ascribing to similar values, particularly in relation to a focus on raising the attainment of disadvantaged learners. Ms E also aligned her school with Clementine's values-driven leadership, which put 'children [and their learning and welfare] at the centre'. For Ms J, this was about preparing students for their futures as 'worthy' and 'productive' members of society. The quote that appears at the beginning of this chapter is worth repeating here:

> In a sense we all have a mission statement, which is to prepare our students for the next stage in their lives, but for us that is recognising that in London, to get a job, to be a worthy and productive member of society, to have an identity, to have choices involves success in exams. It's not empty, it's very real . . . especially for us, given the state of the British economy . . . So, you know, in terms of morality, one of the things that we're most proud of from last year is that . . . every single one of [our sixteen-year-olds] is in [education], productive employment or training. And that's an achievement. And it's an Ofsted measure. And it's not a bad measure.
>
> (Ms J)

Consistent with the previous section, we can see here how broader moral codes or modes of subjection (in this case, external accountabilities in the form of exam results and Ofsted measures) powerfully shape behaviour and actions. These codes constitute what is 'good' preparation 'for the next stage in [students'] lives'. As noted in Chapter 2, education determines employment credentialing and students' subsequent participation in the labour market. Thus, a key platform of socially just schooling must be to prepare students for their future productive participation in this labour market by supporting them to achieve on the measuring sticks (i.e. assessment standards) that count. Ms J recognises this platform when declaring that the 'moral imperative' of 'success in exams' is crucial for 'prepar[ing] students for the next stage in their lives . . . to get a job [and] to have choices'.

While some members of the alliance expressed reservations about working within these codes (these reservations are detailed in the next chapter), they still prioritised raising attainment in relation to them. For many members, the alliance offered an invaluable 'external perspective' in relation to gauging their success or otherwise on these measures (that 'count') towards better supporting their students. As Mr T explained, 'We are working closely with other schools in order to get skills improvement . . . [so that we can] improve exam outputs at key stages 4 and 5.'

The moral codes of external accountability (especially exam results and Ofsted evaluations) were therefore central to the group's telos of social justice in relation to improving student learning. To these ends, as we saw in the previous section, the group embraced formalised parameters mandated or sanctioned by the Department for Education that would support them in this pursuit. One of these was a Quality Assurance Review conducted as part of a broader programme set up by Challenge Partners, a charity run by and for schools to support school collaboration towards school improvement. This review, led by Clementine, was seen as particularly useful in providing schools with evidence to support them in rethinking their practice. It involved a peer-led evaluation of teaching and learning that 'brings together the rigour and professionalism of Ofsted with the care and collaborative approach of a partnership'. Working with Ofsted-trained inspectors, this process involves leaders in the alliance visiting each other's schools, observing practice and analysing performance data (in relation to pupil achievement, teacher performance and leadership) and seeks to identify areas of strength, weakness and future challenge (Challenge Partners, 2012: 14). Ms M's comments were illustrative of the head teachers' opinion of this review process:

> One of the things that I think has been fantastic is the external review
> that we have through the partnership so that we have a quality

assurance review done once a year with senior leaders coming in from another school, and I think that's been really powerful.

(Ms M)

Like Ms M, Mr I expressed his view about the usefulness of this 'external perspective' as a valuable learning opportunity, both to 'reinforce what we are doing here' and to support a rethinking of and improvement in practice. He explained:

Being part of a review team and working closely with an Ofsted inspector . . . [has] sharpened my practice and made me more aware of other schools and of [what the 'goal posts' are] and of making better use of our data [to improve what we do].

(Mr I)

Consistent with the aims of the Challenge Partners programme, Mr I's comments attest to the benefits of working alongside an Ofsted inspector. Evidence from this source about issues of school quality and review seems, for Mr I, to reflect a sense of rigour and professionalism. The moral codes within this approach are clearly construed here as contributing productively to the group's social justice telos of learner improvement. Strategic engagement with these moral codes, as noted in the previous section, was assisted by the group's engagement with accredited programmes, such as the OTP and Challenge the Gap. As with supporting the group's prioritising of autonomy and collaboration, these programmes were seen as similarly helpful in realising the group's telos of learner improvement because they were aimed explicitly at improving the quality of teaching, learning and leadership practices across the alliance.

For the Clementine-led alliance, the moral codes of external performance measures were central to pursuing the group's telos of social justice: that is, supporting improved learning outcomes for all students. For the schools in the alliance, these modes were the indication of whether or not they were providing a 'good' preparation for students' future productive participation in society. Indeed, they reflected, in Ms J's view, the group's moral imperative. Working within these modes was seen as not only moral but strategic. This is unsurprising, given that exam results and Ofsted evaluations are the measures that 'count' for these schools in terms of their survival and future success. Such moral codes – in the form of initiatives such as the Quality Assurance Review and the Outstanding Teacher Programme – were, in this respect, embraced by the group as helping them to pursue their telos of student improvement. Importantly, it seems that working within these codes did not undermine Clementine's leadership focus on fostering the individual autonomy of member schools and collaboration between schools. The Quality Assurance Review supports on-going consultation and evaluation that is peer-led and collaborative while the Outstanding Teacher Programme builds capacity *within* schools by enhancing school-led professional development networks *between* schools. As we saw in the previous section, it appears that these moral parameters were drawn on in productive ways towards school and learner improvement as opposed to blaming and punitive ways.

The positive approach to the modes of subjection shaping the leadership and social justice telos within the alliance is abundantly clear in the head teachers' remarks in this chapter. The productive results of this approach are undeniable. What *is* worrying are the ways in which such modes of subjection are understood and adopted in largely uncritical ways. Indeed, programmes such as the OTP and mechanisms such as the Quality Assurance Review are embraced for the sole purpose of realising the pragmatic performative goals associated with exam results and Ofsted evaluations. While, as we will see in the next chapter, the head teachers expressed reservations about and offer strong critique of the inadequacies of these performative goals and their parameters in measuring school quality, the embracing of the modes of subjection towards achieving them raises some significant concerns. It seems that the sole focus in the alliance on achieving pragmatic performative goals will do little to disrupt the narrow rearticulation of 'quality' teachers and teaching that is hegemonic in the current audit culture. The preoccupation within the alliance with raising achievement leaves little space, it seems, for conversation and development around creative and innovative curricula and pedagogy. More likely, this preoccupation will perpetuate 'one-size-fits-all' delivery models. Such a preoccupation and focus, moreover, seem to be entirely consistent with the re-emphasis in teacher standards and teacher education on 'practicality' and 'relevance'. It seems from the head teachers' remarks in this chapter that practical and experiential knowledge is privileged in their work within the alliance over theoretical, pedagogical and subject knowledge (Beauchamp et al., 2013). Given the broader imperatives within which the alliance is working, this is not unexpected. However, it suggests a taken-for-grantedness around, rather than a critique of, the far from ideologically innocent modes of subjection shaping these head teachers' work.

Conclusion

This chapter introduced seven of the twenty schools within the Clementine-led alliance and their head teachers. These schools were described as wide-ranging in terms of model, type and Ofsted rating, but as reflecting similarly diverse student demographics and similar strong commitments to the alliance and its purpose. Clementine itself is an outstanding academy and teaching school; it leads this alliance and its 'mission' to support all students to achieve educational success. Within the parameters of the National Teaching Schools initiative and external departmental guidelines and accountabilities, Clementine adopted particular leadership practices in this pursuit and a strong articulation of its telos. Its ethical approach to working with the other alliance schools was reflected in its respecting of individual school autonomy and its fostering of collaboration between the schools. While this approach shifted according to various demands and interrelations, certain practices of effective networking were prioritised, such as a rejection of an authoritarian or expert model of leadership and the adoption of commonly agreed structures and programmes for encouraging collaboration and learner improvement. The focus in the alliance on autonomy and collaboration was highly valued by the member schools. Most members seemed to feel that these practices accorded them a voice in decision-making and the freedom and flexibility to take up or reject opportunities within the alliance.

The parameters of accountability or modes of subjection (i.e. exam results and Ofsted measures) powerfully shaped the group's ideas about what constitutes learner improvement. Significant reservations relating to these parameters will be explored in the next chapter. Nevertheless, success in relation to these modes of accountability was construed as key to pursuing the group's mission to prepare students for their future productive participation in the labour market and the alliance was seen as an invaluable 'external perspective' for gauging each school's success (or otherwise) in this regard. To these ends, the group embraced the formalised parameters mandated or sanctioned by the Department for Education that were seen to support them in this pursuit.

In the next chapter, we explore the significance of advocacy, truth-telling and counter-conduct within the Clementine-led alliance. Within the context of the broader pressures of autonomous schooling and the demands of the audit culture, we draw attention to the significance of these practices in Clementine's pursuit of socially just leadership and in member schools negotiating some of the constraints of this leadership.

Note

1 These terminologies and ratings were accurate at the time of data collection in mid-2013.

References

Beauchamp, G., Clarke, L., Hulme, M. and Murray, J. (2013). *Research and teacher education: The BERA–RSA inquiry: Policy and practice within the United Kingdom*. London, British Educational Research Association.

Black-Hawkins, K. (2007). Networking schools. In C. McLaughlin, K. Black-Hawkins, D. McIntyre and A. Townsend (eds) *Networking practitioner research*. Hoboken, NJ, Taylor and Francis.

Challenge Partners (2012). *Challenge Partners introduction pack*. London, Challenge Partners.

Chapman, C., Allen, T. and Harris, A. (2005). *Networked learning communities and schools facing challenging circumstances*. Warwick, University of Warwick Press.

Department for Education (2013). *What is an academy?* From www.education.gov.uk/schools/leadership/typesofschools/academies/b00205692/whatisanacademy, accessed 12 March 2015.

Earl, L. and Katz, S. (2005). *Learning from Networked Learning communities – phase 2 – key features and inevitable tensions*. Toronto, Aporia Consulting.

Foucault, M. (1981). *The history of sexuality*, Volume I. London, Penguin.

Foucault, M. (1992). *The history of sexuality*, Volume II: *The use of pleasure*. Harmondsworth, Penguin.

Foucault, M. (2000). The ethics of the concern for self as a practice of freedom. In P. Rabinow (ed.) *Essential works of Foucault 1954–1984*, Volume I: *Ethics*. London, Penguin.

Fraser, N. (1997). *Justice interruptus: Critical reflections on the 'postsocialist' condition*. New York, Routledge.

Fraser, N. (2009). *Scales of justice: Reimagining political space in a globalizing world*. New York, Columbia University Press.

Glatter, R. (2012). Persistent preoccupations: The rise and rise of school autonomy and accountability in England. *Educational management administration and leadership*, 40 (5), 559–575.

Hargreaves, D. (2011). System redesign for system capacity building. *Journal of Educational Administration*, 49 (6), 685–700.

Hill, R. (2010). *Chain reactions: A thinkpiece on the development of chains of schools in the English school system*. Nottingham, National College for School Leadership.

Hill, R., Dunford, J., Parish, N., Rea, S. and Sandals, R. (2012). *The growth of academy chains: Implications for leaders and leadership*. Nottingham, National College for School Leadership.

Lieberman, A. and McLaughlin, M. W. (1992). Networks for educational change: Powerful and problematic, *Phi Delta Kappan*, May, 673–677.

Muijs, D., Ainscow, M., Chapman, C. and West, M. (2011). *Collaboration and networking in education*. London, Springer.

National College for School Leadership (2011). *National Teaching Schools prospectus*. Nottingham, National College for Teaching and Leadership.

7 Advocacy, truth-telling and counter-conduct as practices of socially just leadership in the Clementine-led alliance

> So, we're in a very challenging climate ... the very survival of schools is at stake ... a very high-stakes system has a lot of very negative consequences [but] one of the positive consequences is that in order to survive it makes you go out there and work with other people. You realise you need to because you cannot do this by yourself. You need to find out how somebody else is making this work in a way that you're not at the moment, and it, ironically, can be a force for good in making schools work more together, collaboratively.
>
> (Mr R)

These comments are from Mr R, the head teacher of the somewhat tired and unkempt – but 'good' – academy described in the previous chapter. His remarks about the significance of school-to-school collaboration reflect the telos of leadership described in Chapter 6. They also encapsulate the broader context of 'challenge' within which this telos must operate and the potential 'negative consequences' of the current 'very high-stakes system'. As explored in the previous chapter and rearticulated here with Mr R's comments, collaboration – or 'working more together' – was welcomed in terms of the support it offered schools to 'survive' in the current climate. However, consistent with the literature detailed in Chapter 2, the head teachers in the alliance expressed concerns about the challenges of school autonomy amid the broader context of 'high-stakes' accountability. These concerns related to:

- a greater autonomised environment increasing both segregation and competition between schools and vulnerability for particular schools; and
- current external measures of school 'success' being inadequate in terms of capturing school quality.

This chapter explores these concerns in relation to matters of leadership and social justice. As in Chapter 5, the focus is on the significance of advocacy, truth-telling and counter-conduct in the alliance's pursuit of its telos of socially just leadership.

Social justice leadership practices

As outlined in Chapter 6, the telos of social justice framing leadership within the Clementine-led alliance prioritises collaboration between schools, autonomy of individual schools and a common focus on improving learning outcomes for all students across the alliance. Pursuing this telos within the challenges and demands of the broader policy environment was, of course, far from simple or straightforward. Alliance members were particularly concerned with the social segregation and inequity generated by systems of school autonomy when driven by external imperatives of accountability and competition (see Boyask, 2010; Lupton, 2011). Such concern is captured in the portraits of the schools offered at the beginning of the previous chapter in the sense that each school's value depends on – and can be reduced to – its Ofsted rating (see Ball, 2003). These ratings segregate schools and pit them against one another. The head teachers relayed their concerns here about how the current autonomised education structure is creating 'vulnerability' within the system, especially for certain schools: for example, small schools, primary schools and schools serving marginalised students (i.e. those that receive lower funds and fewer resources on the basis of student numbers; those that tend not to have sufficient leadership density to improve their school performance; and those that generally cater to students who require greater material and human resource support than the norm; see Ainscow, 2010). Under these conditions, such schools were seen to be 'vulnerable' to the punitive measures associated with 'underperformance'. As Mr R's comments illuminate, their 'very survival . . . is at stake'. Their demographics and circumstances mean that it is impossible for them to compete with more privileged schools and live up to the narrow performative demands of the audit culture (Ball, 2003; West and Ylönen, 2010; Glatter, 2012). Mr R elaborated on the vulnerability of particular schools in the present system:

> Everything is thrown up in the air . . . no one quite knows how it's going to fall . . . What's going to be interesting is what happens when all the schools are converted to academies. So far, unless they've been sponsored, academies are relatively successful schools. But we all know that schools like this are always fragile, because we've got challenging demographics and, you know, these are not

easy institutions to make work. They're very hard to build and they're very easy to destroy. See you get a change in leadership, you get a change in governance or whatever, and some of these schools that have been doing quite well can suddenly not be doing quite well . . . when schools begin to struggle, which they will, inevitably, what's going to happen to those schools? Because, when you've got no local authority, who will be there to pick up the pieces and who will be there to put in the support when they begin to struggle? . . . It is scary . . . They've destroyed the local authority system, which was far from perfect, but it's much easier to destroy something than to build something new.

(Mr R)

Here, Mr R challenges the 'destroying' of 'the local authority system'. He indicates that such destruction is an abrogation of the government's responsibility to support struggling schools (see Lupton, 2011). He also expresses uncertainty about how this displacement of state responsibility will play out through his questioning of how these schools will be supported in the absence of local government intervention within a context of uncertainty and high stakes. In this context, schools, especially those with 'challenging demographics', are 'fragile', 'hard to build' but 'easy to destroy'. Mr R suggests (consistent with the views of many of the alliance's head teachers and the literature more broadly) that this system will privilege the existence and maintenance of 'successful' schools while leaving 'less successful' schools vulnerable and struggling (see Glatter, 2012).

Of course, what is meant by success here, as noted in the previous chapter, is associated with Ofsted evaluations and other standardised measures of school achievement, and the alliance certainly offered members invaluable support in improving their performance on these measures. However, both the validity and the narrowness of these measures were challenged by the head teachers, who shared Mr R's concerns about the high stakes associated with current accountability regimes:

I think it's a bit out of control in terms of the stakes, you know, they want to measure everything, and not everything can be measured . . . there are real dangers in the way the stakes have been constructed.

(Mr R)

Along these lines, the head teachers questioned the validity of the information drawn upon in creating the 'stakes': that is, not everything can be measured. Mr R's reference to the 'dangers' of these stakes is associated with the way in which they generate school vulnerability and, in particular, how they position 'struggling' schools. Such schools (many of which serve deprived communities) are vulnerable to falling behind on standardised measures, such as Ofsted evaluations, which could lead to them being forced to close or be 'taken over'. Such vulnerability, moreover, as Mr R noted in his previous remarks, is often compounded by factors beyond the control of schools, such as challenging and changing student demographics or a change in school leadership or governance – contextual circumstances that tend not to be accounted for in such measures.

In the alliance, working ethically within this climate involved Clementine taking on an advocacy role to support these schools. Clementine's powerful position within and beyond the alliance in terms of its status as an 'outstanding' and leading school enabled such advocacy and the confidence to challenge the stakes through practices of counter-conduct. As with Carol's leadership at Ridgeway (see Chapter 5), such counter-conduct involved truth-telling (parrhesia). For instance, Clementine challenged departmental imperatives and, in particular, the validity of Ofsted evaluation processes. Counter-conduct was also a key practice within the alliance, and was evident in member schools challenging Clementine's leadership in terms of its take up of the standardisation and enterprise practices within the National Teaching Schools initiative. Some member schools rejected these practices as they were articulated in Clementine's relations within the group as undermining their autonomy and choice.

The lead school as advocate, a form of 'political subjectivity'

For some of the head teachers in the alliance, the shift to an increasingly autonomised system was a concern because it amplified school segregation through, for example, a proliferation of 'specialised' schooling models and types. Ms J, for instance, expressed concern that an increase in faith-specific schools was a threat to the multi-cultural and multi-faith richness of de-segregated contexts, such as her own school. Concerns were also expressed about schools becoming increasingly selective in terms of their student intake. For example, Ms E relayed her distress about schools' increasing control over their own admissions. She spoke of 'a number of schools [she knew of] who. . . find all manner of excuses and deliberately falsify their admissions to reject children who are vulnerable', despite the 'lure' of extra funds for these (invariably class) disadvantaged students through the government's Pupil Premium scheme. Mr I's concerns about school autonomy and its production of social segregation and inequity also related to issues of student admissions. He noted that public transparency in terms of the 'massive focus' on the Pupil Premium and free school meals could inadvertently reinscribe class privilege, as he explained:

> If you are an aspirational or affluent parent, you now have that free school meals figure right in your face and, for example, here, we're 55 per cent free school meals ... now, if you are an affluent school parent, are you going to send your kid to a school with 55 per cent free school meals or [to one with] 20 per cent free school meals? ... I think it will unwittingly make us more – the more free school meals will become [even] more free school meals, and the less will become less.
>
> (Mr I)

These concerns that school autonomy may reinforce and reproduce social inequities through increasing educational segregation and hierarchy seem to be well founded. Certainly, consistent with Ms E's and Mr I's remarks, there are fears that schools' greater autonomy over such areas as admissions, coupled with greater parental choice, will reinforce the 'tiering' that is already a sharp feature of the English system. As we noted in Chapter 2, within a competitive market, where funding for schools is based on student numbers, student difference on the basis of social factors such as academic ability and class becomes commodified and accentuated (Glatter, 2009; Lupton, 2011; West and Ylönen, 2010).

Against the backdrop of these concerns, there was much discussion in our interviews about how the segregation and competition encouraged within the current system might begin to be remedied towards better supporting vulnerable students and schools, especially given the head teachers' prediction that local authority support for schools will eventually be eliminated entirely. For instance, Ms E was particularly keen to create and maintain supportive networks with other schools, both primary and secondary, given the vulnerability of her own small and under-resourced primary school and the lack of local authority leadership:

> You suddenly find that there is no local authority left, and we're nearly in that situation [here in this borough]. There's absolutely no leadership from the centre. Primary schools in particular are used to being led by somebody strong [who] then flag[s] the way for you, and [that] has always been the local authority's role.
>
> (Ms E)

As noted earlier, an important imperative of the National Teaching Schools initiative is for lead schools to support schools in need – and particularly schools that Ofsted deems 'require improvement'

(DfE, 2013). At Clementine, this imperative was described as a 'moral' obligation. As a 'strong school', according to Ms S, Clementine was 'morally obliged' to support 'weak schools'. For example, in relation to its concerns about primary schools in the alliance (many of which, as noted in the previous chapter, had not converted to academy status and thus still depended on increasingly limited local authority support), Clementine assumed an advocacy role in terms of applying for funding to support them and creating conditions in which they might retain their autonomy and independence (given that some feared being taken over by chains). Ms S's and Ms J's remarks were illustrative:

> There isn't the critical funding there to enable the local authority to do much really . . . at the moment, for example, they've got an innovation fund, and we put in a bid, because we're a strong school and we've got a track record. We got money which we will now, with the local authority, make sure we target at the needy [i.e. primary] schools.
>
> (Ms S)

> I imagine we'll end up in an 'umbrella trust' with some of our primary schools because they don't want to get swallowed up by the chains, that's how they see it . . . and we're happy to support that when we have quite an aggressive neighbouring secondary school, which we don't regard to be moral [because it is] expansionistic . . . So we would make umbrella trusts to protect them . . . [so that they can] retain their independence and autonomy. It's [also] protecting ourselves. They [the aggressive secondary school] are looking to take our intake, and where we've developed relationships with the school over ten years, and put in teachers to help develop their teaching and learning, we're not so happy if they swan off to this other school.
>
> (Ms J)

Prioritising financial and moral support for the primary schools in the alliance in this way is an example of forms of elaboration exercised by Clementine working within the broader parameters or modes of subjection of the National Teaching Schools initiative. Like Carol at Ridgeway (Chapter 5), Ms S and Ms J constitute themselves as political subjects engaging in highly ethical decisions that form their subjectivities in particular ways. Such ways might, as with Carol, be interpreted as a form of counter-conduct in Clementine's resistance towards, and action to ameliorate, some of the negative impacts of the autonomised system for particular schools (Foucault, 2007). It is important to remember that

Foucault theorised counter-conduct not simply against unpalatable practices or discourses but rather to analyse points of resistance within the spaces in these particular fields.

However it may be interpreted, Clementine's actions were most welcome. Ms E (the primary school head teacher), for example, was highly appreciative of the varied support her school received from Clementine, from subsidising staff to enable their participation in professional development to providing financial support for excursions. This support, in Ms E's words, meant that some of her school's 'big ideas' didn't 'peter out' through lack of resources.

The development of an umbrella trust for primary schools, mentioned by Ms J, involves a group of schools working together under an overarching charitable trust and further exemplifies Clementine working ethically within the parameters of the National Teaching Schools initiative. Such parameters allow for a group of primary schools, which already have a relationship or a similar ethos, to convert to academy status as part of an umbrella trust. The benefits of this model are that these schools retain their autonomy but have input in, and access to, shared governance, collaboration and procurement of services (DfE, 2013). Given the fear of being 'swallowed up by chains' (a fear confirmed by Ms E, who expressed ideological opposition to the idea of academies and academy chains), this would seem to be a useful structure not only to help this school's survival and protect its autonomy but also to generate connection and cooperation within the alliance. Of course, as Ms J's remarks make clear, Clementine does not lose out under such an arrangement – it is an investment in relationships and collaboration that ensures and protects this school's intake and, in turn, its income.

There is recognition here that the current system generates conditions where some schools – on account of, for example, their small size or high proportion of students with significant learning needs – are unable to participate on par with other better-resourced or more privileged schools (Fraser, 1997). As noted earlier, in a competitive market where funding to schools is based on student numbers, student difference based on social factors such as academic ability and class becomes commodified and accentuated (see West and Ylönen, 2010). In this climate, less desirable students (i.e. those who do not achieve well on external tests and who are invariably class and race disadvantaged) are marginalised. This marginalisation in the present climate is captured in Ms E's reports of schools falsifying their admissions to reject such students. Mr I notes similar marginalisation within the system associated with issues of poverty, with aspirational or affluent parents averse to sending their children to schools that receive higher than average economic support in the form of free school meals.

Clementine's commitment as a 'strong school' is to support the weaker schools in the alliance through removing some of the barriers (economic and political) impeding these schools' capacity to thrive amid broader performative demands (Fraser, 2009). Its advocacy role on behalf of the primary schools in the alliance illustrates this commitment. Economic support as a form of elaboration is provided in Clementine applying for funding to subsidise particular activities within these schools, such as professional development and excursions. Political support is offered in Clementine's intentions to set up an umbrella trust for the primary schools to ensure that they retain their autonomy and independence. Being 'swallowed up' by chains is seen as certain to undermine these schools' political agency and decision-making power. Within the accountability demands of the current climate, the adoption of these redistributive and representative principles may alleviate some of the injustices generated by the academies programme. As noted earlier, within this programme, 'outstanding' schools (which tend to be well resourced and well supported) are given autonomy, a voice and (at least in the past) financial incentives. These schools are able to choose to become academies, gaining the power and control that come with this status. Underperforming schools, on the other hand (which tend to be less well resourced and supported, and cater to less privileged student cohorts), tend to lose power and control under this programme. They are susceptible to punitive external accountability measures, such as losing status, students and funding due to falls in their Ofsted rating, or losing autonomy when they are instructed to work under a sponsor (DfE, 2013).

Clementine's support of vulnerable schools can therefore be seen as working to dismantle some of the injustices within the system that privilege some schools while marginalising others. Supporting these vulnerable schools is especially important given the dismantling of the local authority. It would appear then, that alliances such as the one led by Clementine will (in the words of Mr R) 'be there to pick up the pieces' and 'put in the support when [schools] begin to struggle' without the safety net of a local authority.

Against this backdrop, we can see that Clementine is working ethically and justly within the parameters of the National Teaching Schools initiative. What is concerning, however, are the ways in which the ethics of these parameters – and structures such as umbrella trusts – remain unchallenged. For example, there is no recognition or critique of how these parameters might be seen as ethically unsound and profoundly unjust by playing into and strengthening the broader ideologies of the 'Big Society' and helping to create a market-oriented and undemocratic education system.

Leadership and counter-conduct

While, as we saw earlier, external accountability measures such as Ofsted evaluations and other standardised measures of school achievement were key indicators of what the alliance considered 'quality' and 'success', these measures were strongly challenged by some of the head teachers. In particular, as Mr R's earlier comments illustrate, there was a questioning of their narrowness and validity in capturing and representing school quality and of their promotion of competition rather than collaboration. Such questioning was reflected in various forms of counter-conduct at the local school level (Foucault, 1981). Like Carol's practices of counter-conduct at Ridgeway (described in Chapter 5), the leaders in the Clementine-led alliance similarly engaged in parrhesia by speaking out against what they saw as unjust and inadequate departmental evaluation processes. There was a risk involved in speaking out in relation to the differential status of the speaker (Clementine) and the audience (Ofsted inspectors and officials). However, the leaders at Clementine, like Carol at Ridgeway, designated importance to speaking their truth rather than letting the status quo continue unchallenged. Foucault (2012) makes specific reference to the importance of the relationship between the speaker and others. This is not simply a one-way transmission of truth-telling but a more symbiotic relationship in which the 'listener' plays an active role for the truth-teller in their formation of the self as a political subject. This is where the risk exists for the truth-teller: for instance, in this high-stakes world of education there are risks associated with speaking out against ratings, inspections, status and funding for Clementine. For Foucault, 'a form of courage' is required because the risk will potentially offend the other individual or group. It may irritate them, make them angry, or even provoke them to violent conduct (Foucault, 2012). As Foucault (2012: 11) argues, 'the parrhesiast always risks undermining that relationship which is the condition of possibility of his discourse'.

Performing well on Ofsted measures is, of course, very important. As noted earlier, it represents extremely high stakes for schools and staff. While not in any way rejecting the notion of accountability, the leaders at Clementine (especially Ms J and her assistant, Ms C) were very critical of the processes involved in their recent Ofsted evaluation. In particular, they challenged the Ofsted inspectors' insufficient expertise and skills to adequately carry out an evaluation of the school. This inadequacy of expertise was salient for Ms J and Ms C in relation to a lack of cultural and religious knowledge and sensitivities as the following examples illustrate:

> I'm more than happy to be accountable . . . I just don't think we should be judged by people who are quite so . . . well, who didn't

know what they were looking at, [especially] when you look at what was at stake for us . . . Our head boy [is] a refugee . . . [a] black African – target grades for A level, target university Imperial, which is one of our very best for Physics. I mean, that's an amazing achievement for anybody, in whatever route they came to education, and [one of the inspectors] kept asking him what exposure he's had to gang warfare . . . We have a comedian [who says,] 'Is it cos I is black? Would you have asked me that question if I had been white?'

(Ms J)

[There] was one particular RE lesson that was observed by one particular inspector . . . The teacher had decided to do a lesson on the difference between the Old and New Testaments, because not many of our pupils would know about that . . . Only – what? – 17 per cent of our mix is white, let alone if it's Christian and white . . . So she planned it all and she was sort of pulled up for it being too basic a lesson. Surely everyone in Britain knew the difference between the Old and New Testaments? Which is a huge assumption!

(Ms C)

The cultural and religious essentialisms deployed in these examples highlight a dissonance between the knowledge and sensitivities of the inspectors and the knowledge and sensitivities that would support an informed and productive analysis of Clementine as a highly complex multicultural and multi-faith context. Such essentialisms conflate blackness with gang warfare, and Britishness with (Christian) knowledge of the Old and New Testaments. Alongside these concerns, Ms J and Ms C found the inadequacy of the inspection process highly problematic. In Ms J's words, the inspection was not 'fit for purpose'.

Although the school received an 'outstanding' grade – and, in Ms J's words, a 'lovely Ofsted report' – Clementine took immediate action to bring this issue to the attention of Ofsted's chief inspector, Michael Wilshaw, and the chair of the Ofsted Board:

So have we taken action? Yes . . . [our executive] head is very, very political here and so she's phoned Michael Wilshaw already, [and she's] spoken to Sally Morgan, who is his boss, so she's working at a variety of levels to [alert people about] the process going on, which isn't fit for purpose.

(Ms J)

These criticisms and actions towards Ofsted suggest a sense of confidence and assertiveness that can be attributed, at least in part, to the school's high status in the education community and its position as a lead school within the National Teaching Schools initiative. Clementine's willingness to practise parrhesia as well as the outcomes arising from it must be seen within this context. It is likely, for example, that a school with lower status and less 'credibility' would be less likely to engage in such 'fearless speech' (Foucault, 2001). Nevertheless, there is certainly still an element of risk in such engagement, which relates to the difference in status between Clementine and Ofsted. Such risk-taking illustrates the importance Clementine's leaders place on challenging a status quo that is inadequate, and misleading and not 'fit for purpose' to use Ms J's words. Like Carol's engagement in parrhesia, this challenging exemplifies Foucault's idea of power as productive and working in an ascending manner (1981). Moreover, and illustrating Clementine's prioritising of an ethical and just approach to leadership (i.e. its concern beyond itself to the fairness and impact of external accountabilities in principle), the school engaged in parrhesia despite receiving 'a lovely Ofsted report' and a grade of 'outstanding'.

The other significant ways in which counter-conduct operated within the alliance related to individual schools protecting their autonomy. This involved some of the head teachers challenging or resisting aspects of Clementine's leadership. There were requirements of enterprise and standardisation embedded in the National Teaching Schools initiative that were seen by some head teachers as potentially thwarting the group's telos of collaboration, respect for autonomy and focus on improving learning for all students.

As noted earlier, Clementine, as a teaching school, receives government funding for three years to lead and build capacity within the alliance in relation to improving teaching, learning and leadership. However, it is also expected to be enterprising in generating further income to sustain its programmes and the employment of extra staff whose job it is to manage these programmes (National College for School Leadership, 2011). Several of the alliance members expressed unease at this compunction for Clementine to be enterprising. Ms E's remarks were illustrative:

> If you're set up to be, in the end, self-funding, your moral imperative is compromised because you've got to say to yourself, 'actually, this is a money-spinner, we'll do it' . . . and I think there is a tension . . . so I do think Clementine [is] going to be compromised . . . It is pressurised, terribly pressurised . . . When you've got to be self-funding to exist, you might have to make compromises that you weren't intending to make and it sticks in your craw, you know, like. I can see that.
>
> (Ms E)

Consistent with comments in the previous chapter about Clementine being a 'values-driven' organisation, the general view was that the alliance leadership was not compromised by enterprising imperatives. However, a few of the head teachers mentioned specific examples where such imperatives were salient in their dealings with Clementine in ways that could potentially undermine more educationally focused agendas, such as improving learning outcomes and fostering collaborative school-to-school relations. Ms M, for example, expressed discomfort that in heads' meetings at Clementine, 'there tends to be somebody trying to sell you something', while Mr T's concerns about the dangers of market imperatives on relations within the alliance were more detailed:

> Clementine has a very strong position as an 'outstanding' school and a teaching school . . . now the danger is that [with this position] you get money, you get that entrepreneurial buzz that comes from the money and you keep feeding that rather than feeding the need to improve student outcomes . . . I'm not saying Clementine is doing that consciously, but I think subconsciously they might be . . .
>
> It becomes the 'Clementine Show' sometimes . . . It does feel sometimes like Clementine's agenda is sort of forced on us . . . I don't mind some of the 'making us aware' stuff [because some things are really useful, but] . . . I think what happens is people approach Clementine in order to try and market certain services through Clementine, and then Clementine ends up pushing that through the alliance and they become, if they're not careful . . . a little bit like a supermarket that's just collecting a lot of goods and flogging them to a local audience. I don't want that. What I want those meetings to be is discussions about how we improve outcomes for our kids . . . I don't want it to be a sales pitch that's just a waste of my time.
>
> (Mr T)

These comments illustrate a key tension confronting Clementine. While clearly prioritising the educational imperative of improving learning outcomes for all students, this school must also prioritise economic imperatives, especially in its enterprising role as a 'teaching school'. Working within these modes of subjection seems to generate tensions and the possibility of detracting from an educational focus – instilling an 'entrepreneurial buzz that comes from money' and forcing a 'sales' agenda of 'flogging' 'goods' 'like a supermarket'. For Ms E, Ms M and Mr T, the conflict between these two imperatives was clear. Mr T provided a specific example:

> There's a [teacher improvement] programme that we could buy through the alliance which would cost us a significant amount of

money. We've put our own together and we've saved ourselves a lot of money, but we keep getting this sort of programme thrust at us through the alliance . . . My view is I've got outstanding teachers at [this] school and the best way for my teachers who are not outstanding to become outstanding is to work with those outstanding teachers.

(Mr T)

This could be viewed as an instance when Clementine's ethics have been compromised by the imperative to generate income. A focus on the ideologies of enterprise and business can be seen here as overriding and compromising educative goals (see Gunter, 2012). We might contrast this with Mr T's efforts to reconcile the tensions between the two. His development of his own programme is economically efficient while also working to improve the quality of his teachers and making better use of the existing expertise in his school within the particular requirements of his school context (Muijs et al., 2011). Such an approach can be seen as a form of counter-conduct along similar lines to Carol's non-compliance with the expectations of the *Leadership Matters* framework detailed in Chapter 5. Rather than ascribing uncritically to the offerings of the alliance, Mr T works in autonomous ways to protect the interests of his school (Foucault, 2000). This is where there are spaces within the alliance for individuals and schools to act and exercise forms of counter-conduct. Mr T is exercising his own form of counter-conduct in relation to both mandated policy arrangements *and* the political structures of the alliance.

Along similar lines to Mr T's concerns, there were other practices of counter-conduct relating to the teacher improvement programmes promoted through the alliance. Some alliance members saw some of these programmes as reductionist and inflexible. Their one-size-fits-all approach was seen as inappropriate for some schools. To be sure, the current climate tends to encourage this reductionism through the increasing imperative for schools to follow business principles, which involve standardising and commodifying interventions and practices through specific norms of quality assurance and validation. This approach was 'restrictive', according to Ms E. She explained this restrictiveness specifically in relation to the Outstanding Teacher Programme: 'We [felt it was] a little bit dated, [but] we weren't allowed to adapt it really. We did adapt it, but had we been quality assured we probably would have had our knuckles rapped.'

In line with these and other remarks quoted earlier, Clementine's project manager, Ms S, did stress the significance of financial enterprise and viability in the selection and management of programmes for the alliance as well as the imperative for programmes to be standardised so that they could be quality assured. According to Ms S, the programmes offered needed to align with both educational and economic imperatives. They needed to focus on improving the quality of leadership, teaching and learning across all schools in the alliance, while also netting an economic return for Clementine so as not to drain the resources of the 'mother ship'. She further explained:

> The two arms are financially viable programmes and developing really effective practice, which is costly . . . People like me are not cheap . . . It's got to be financially viable so that what I call the 'mother ship', which is Clementine, doesn't financially and resource-wise dissipate its strength. Clementine's in the position it is because it's an outstanding school . . . The alliance should strengthen all the schools without being a drain purely on Clementine.
>
> (Ms S)

Ms S's use of the term 'mother ship' is interesting, as Foucault (1991) uses the example of captaining a ship to illustrate his notion of government. For instance, he explains how this involves not only taking charge of the sailors on the ship but also bringing the cargo safely to port through the many dangers at sea. This is done through establishing a relationship with the sailors and the boat and its cargo. Foucault (1991: 93) describes government as the 'complex composed of men and things'. This is not necessarily how Ms S views the work at Clementine, but Foucault's notion of governmentality is helpful in terms of understanding the relationship between the 'mother ship' and the other schools in the alliance and the distribution and management of people and resources.

The financial viability of programmes in terms of their capacity to generate an economic return was associated with quality assurance and standardisation. Indeed, the standardisation of programmes seemed to be equated with guarantees that they could deliver predictable quality outcomes for schools (through such standardisation). Ms S remarked for example:

> In the past we weren't precious about intellectual property and we were probably less rigorous on [or worried about] sharing knowledge, so you would see a programme somewhere and [you would] adapt it and run it differently in your own school. But if you're going to ask people to pay, our large heads are saying we want quality assurance. We want to know, if we're going to go on this programme, that it's got this label and that it will deliver this outcome.
>
> (Ms S)

These anxieties about protecting intellectual property and the 'rigour' of knowledge in programmes are products of the current climate. In this climate, embracing the business principles of standardising and commodifying interventions and practices through specific norms of quality assurance and validation is central to schools' survival and success (Ball, 2003; Maguire et al., 2011). These are powerful modes of subjection that shape how, in this case, Clementine balances its 'two arms' of 'financially viable programmes' and 'effective practice'. The counter-conduct of Mr T and Ms E suggests that Clementine does not always get this balance right. For these head teachers, the standardising and commodifying of resources do not assure quality and do not necessarily lead to effectiveness or success, especially because these processes cannot be sufficiently responsive to context. In Mr T's case, such programmes were not conducive to recognising and building on the skills and expertise already working well in his school. Moreover, in his view, Clementine 'flogs' them to the other schools, which is clearly at odds with the leadership telos of collaboration and respect for autonomy within the alliance. According to Ms E, at least one of the programmes is 'dated' and needed modification. In both cases, these head teachers' counter-conduct involved engaging with alternatives to what is offered, with Mr T developing his own teacher improvement programme and Ms E adapting the OTP to suit the particular circumstances of her school.

Also consistent with the aims of the National Teaching Schools initiative, Clementine's approach to 'strengthening' the alliance was to build capacity. An aspect of this was to encourage other schools to assume leadership roles within particular programmes. While such encouragement was intended to enrich collaborations between schools, it seemed to have had the opposite effect for some of the schools who were resistant to being involved. A lack of economic and material resources was a key factor in this resistance. The heads from several of the schools, for example, did not feel that their school was currently equipped in terms of human and material capacity and resources to assume leadership roles and felt that they needed to 'strengthen' their schools before accepting such roles. Ms M noted, for example, that she didn't believe her school was a 'steady enough ship to start sorting everybody else out'. Mr I commented similarly:

> One of the key things that we've been asked to do is to be a lead school next year in [one of the programmes offered] . . . What we want to do . . . instead of leading other schools [is] consolidate [here] . . . We really need to consolidate . . . It's all right for schools in Clementine's situation, an 'outstanding' school, but we're in a different situation and we have to help *our* students . . . You need to have

a think about the context you work in. We are a school ['requiring improvement']. We haven't got the staffing capacity. I need my good teachers working here, not going off to work in another school.

(Mr I)

As with earlier quotes from Mr T and Ms E, the counter-conduct here relates to Ms M and Mr I attempting to protect their autonomy within the alliance and ensure that alliance activities and duties are sensitive and appropriate to their own individual contexts. Similar to Clementine's truth-telling with respect to its Ofsted evaluation, there is a recognition here of the differential status between the speaker (Ms M's school or Mr I's school) and the audience (Clementine); and perhaps here, too, there is a risk involved in these head teachers speaking out against Clementine's request for them to become 'lead schools'. Clementine is clearly in a position of power in terms of its greater status as a teaching school and leader of the alliance, but also in terms of its greater material resources and capacity. Such a position certainly means Clementine has the potential to undermine these other schools' sense of autonomy and equitable collaboration. This is where Clementine must continue to work on itself in order to govern effectively and work with the other schools in the alliance. This is not simply a top-down flow of power but power as inscribed in the practices exercised by Clementine and also by the schools as forms of counter-conduct to Clementine's modes of governmentality.

Major tensions between Clementine and the other alliance schools are obvious here, and they are likely to compromise genuinely collaborative relations and detract from a focus on students and learning. Certainly, capacity-building and encouraging leadership within the alliance are highly positive and productive moves on Clementine's part. However, as Ms M's and Mr I's comments indicate, these moves may undermine the autonomy and collaboration that Clementine positions as central to leading in ethical ways as well as its efforts to lead in contextually relevant and responsive ways. Moreover, it is clear that the wider distribution of leadership tasks is not an entirely altruistic move on Clementine's part. It is partly driven by economic imperatives. Distributing leadership throughout the alliance means that Clementine will be less likely to find its resources stretched. These resources are, of course, crucial if the school is to maintain its 'outstanding' status.

While, as a 'strong' school and a teaching school, Clementine is expected to offer support to the other members of the alliance, as Ms S noted the danger for Clementine is that such provision may act as a 'drain' on its own resources. The economic and political remedies adopted by Clementine require significant human and material resourcing and they shift focus from the school itself. Clementine, along with all other schools both within and beyond the alliance, is operating within the confines of the broader high-stakes environment as modes of subjection. Hence, it is under enormous pressure to 'look good' (or, in Clementine's case, *continue* to look good) in line with this environment (Ball, 2003; Maguire et al., 2011). As a senior member of staff (from the broader study) at Clementine noted: 'the pressure that schools are under, especially academies like ours, is huge . . . The pressure is that you've done really well, you've got "outstanding", [but] if you dip then you lose everything.' For Clementine, looking good is about maintaining the school's 'outstanding' status. Any dip would mean that it would lose its teaching school status. Clementine's concerns with resource efficiency, financial viability and the dispersion of leadership responsibility throughout the alliance are clearly warranted amid the pressure of this high-stakes environment. Were it not to prioritise these aspects of leadership, the 'mother ship' would indeed 'dissipate its strength' (Ms S).

This focus on enterprise may compromise Clementine's ethical ways of leading and undermine its efforts to support school autonomy and independence, as Mr T's comments about Clementine acting a 'bit like a supermarket' attest. The pressure on it to peddle 'money spinners' (Ms E) or standardised resources that are not appropriate for all schools within the alliance not only sidelines student learning outcomes but may also silence voices within the alliance, compromising their input into decision-making about what might be good and appropriate for their individual contexts.

Other schools in the alliance, of course, are equally driven by economic imperatives. They feel that their resources and capacity, unlike Clementine's, do not equip them to accept greater responsibilities within the alliance, such as more leadership roles, and believe that their quality of provision for students will be compromised should they take up such roles. Mr I's remarks are instructive here in drawing attention to the significance of context in shaping how schools understand and navigate these imperatives – in this climate, 'outstanding' and well-resourced schools like Clementine are better able to 'lead' and 'consolidate' than 'satisfactory' and less well-resourced schools (see Braun et al., 2011).

It is perhaps heartening to see in the examples of counter-conduct among the alliance schools a questioning of the parameters of the National Teaching Schools initiative. There is a recognition that these parameters can play out in ethically unsound and unjust ways, as well as a challenging of their market-oriented agenda and their tendency towards undemocratic relations. The alliance schools' counter-conduct illustrates an awareness of the limitations of the standardised, prescriptive and decontextualised frames for what might constitute teacher quality and improvement that are offered through the alliance within the parameters of the National Teaching Schools initiative. In light of such limitations, these schools seek alternatives that respond better to their specific require-ments. These alternatives (while still usually focused on performative goals) generally seem to be educative, rather than enterprising, in focus. Importantly, they reflect a willingness to challenge the current re-emphasis within teaching and teacher quality on 'practicality' and 'relevance' (Beauchamp et al., 2013). They open the space for understand-ing teaching as a complex, situated and intellectual activity rather than a set of skills that can be prescribed, quantified and evaluated. Against this backdrop, we can see how such counter-conduct might begin to disrupt the market-centred and undemocratic ideologies that are perpetuated through the broader 'Big Society' ideology framing English education.

Conclusion

This chapter has explored the significance of advocacy, truth-telling and counter-conduct within the Clementine-led alliance in terms of pursuing its telos of socially just leadership. Such practices were mobilised in an attempt to ameliorate some of the negative impacts of the broader policy context as modes of subjection: namely, the increasing segregation and competition between schools and the vulnerability of particular schools generated by a greater autonomised environment; and the inadequacy of current external accountabilities as valid indicators of school success and quality.

Clementine's ethical approach to this situation was one of advocacy for 'vulnerable' schools in the alliance it leads. Within the parameters of the National Teaching Schools initiative, Clementine provided financial and moral support to ensure that these schools could retain their auton-omy and independence. While one might (indeed *should*) question the ethical soundness of these parameters, such support was interpreted as a form of counter-conduct in Clementine's resistance towards, and action to ameliorate, some of the barriers (economic and political) impeding these schools' capacity to thrive amid broader performative demands.

In further reference to practices of counter-conduct, there was a strong challenging of the external accountabilities measuring school perfor-mance. Such measures, especially Ofsted evaluations, were challenged for their inadequacy in capturing and representing school quality. Counter-conduct was also a key practice *within* the alliance and this was evident in member schools challenging aspects of Clementine's leadership. Rather than ascribing uncritically to the offerings of the alliance, these schools engaged with alternatives that were more responsive to the needs of their particular contexts and protected the interests of their schools. Such counter-conduct, importantly, questioned the ethical parameters of the

National Teaching Schools initiative: for example, their tendency to lead to undemocratic relations and their mandate to promote standardised, prescriptive and decontextualised frames for teacher quality and improvement. We argue that counter-conduct in the form of schools developing alternatives to these parameters is important in beginning to disrupt the more harmful 'Big Society' ideologies that currently frame English education.

In the next chapter, we draw on the book's theoretical tools to bring together specific points of resonance across the two case studies. Our explicit engagement is with the ethical dimensions of leadership and especially Foucault's ideas of truth-telling, counter-conduct and advocacy, and their utility in generating spaces through which socially just leadership can flourish.

References

Ainscow, M. (2010). Achieving excellence and equity: Reflections on the development of practices in one local district over 10 years. *School Effectiveness and School Improvement*, 21 (1) 75–92.

Ball, S. (2003). The teacher's soul and the terrors of performativity. *Journal of Education Policy*, 18 (2), 215–228.

Beauchamp, G., Clarke, L., Hulme, M. and Murray, J. (2013). *Research and teacher education: The BERA–RSA inquiry: Policy and practice within the United Kingdom*. London, British Educational Research Association.

Boyask, R. (2010). Individuality, equity and free schooling in the twenty-first century. Keynote paper presented at the International Sociology of Education Conference, London, 5–7 November.

Braun, A., Ball, S., Maguire, M. and Hoskins, K. (2011). Taking context seriously: Towards explaining policy enactments in the secondary school. *Discourse: Studies in the Politics of Education*, 32, 585–596.

Department for Education (DfE) (2013). *What is an academy?* From http://www.education.gov.uk/schools/leadership/typesofschools/academies/b00205692/whatisanacademy, accessed 11 March 2015.

Foucault, M. (1981). *The history of sexuality*, Volume I. London, Penguin.

Foucault, M. (1991). Governmentality. In G. Burchill, C. Gordon and P. Miller (eds) *The Foucault effect: Studies in governmentality*. Chicago, University of Chicago Press.

Foucault, M. (2000). The ethics of the concern for self as a practice of freedom. In. P. Rabinow (ed.) *Essential works of Foucault 1954–1984*, Volume I: *Ethics*. London, Penguin.

Foucault, M. (2001). *Fearless speech*. Edited by J. Pearson. Los Angeles, CA, Semiotext(e).

Foucault, M. (2007). *Security, territory, population: Lectures at the College de France 1977–1978*. New York, Picador.

Foucault, M. (2012). *The courage of truth (the government of self and others 2): Lectures at the College de France 1983–1984*. New York, Picador.

Fraser, N. (1997). *Justice interruptus: Critical reflections on the 'postsocialist' condition*. New York, Routledge.

Fraser, N. (2008). Reframing justice in a globalising world. In K. Olson (ed.) *Adding insult to injury: Nancy Fraser debates her critics*. London, Verso.

Fraser, N. (2009). *Scales of justice: Re-imagining political space in a globalizing world*. New York, Columbia University Press.

Glatter, R. (2009). Let's look at academies systemically. *Management in Education*, 23 (3), 104–107.

Glatter, R. (2012). Persistent preoccupations: The rise and rise of school autonomy and accountability in England. *Educational Management Administration and Leadership*, 40 (5), 559–575.

Gunter, H. (2012). *Leadership and the reform of education*. Bristol, Policy Press.

Lingard, B. and Sellar, S. (2012). A policy sociology reflection on school reform in England: From the 'Third Way' to the 'Big Society'. *Journal of Educational Administration and History*, 44 (1), 43–63.

Lupton, R. (2011). 'No change there then!' The onward march of school markets and competition. *Journal of Educational Administration and History*, 43 (4), 309–323.

Maguire, M., Perryman, J., Ball, S. and Braun, A. (2011). The ordinary school: What is it? *British Journal of Sociology of Education*, 32 (1), 1–16.

Muijs, D., Ainscow, M., Chapman, C. and West, M. (2011). *Collaboration and networking in education*. London, Springer.

National College for School Leadership (2011). *National Teaching Schools prospectus*. Nottingham, National College for Teaching and Leadership.

West, A. and Ylönen, A. (2010). Market-oriented school reform in England and Finland: School choice, finance and governance. *Educational Studies*, 36 (1), 1–12.

8   Conclusion
Leadership, ethics and schooling for social justice

Ridgeway is a low-performing state high school situated in suburban Queensland. It is a relatively small school that caters to a high proportion of very poor students who are from a broader community that is troubled by violence, crime and culturally driven conflict. The security at Ridgeway is tight, with twenty-four-hour video surveillance cameras dotted about its grounds and two Rottweiler dogs patrolling at night. The Clementine Academy, by contrast, is a high-performing school situated in a London borough. It is so 'outstanding' that it is charged with leading an alliance of twenty schools. Large and well resourced with teaching occurring in friendly learning huts, it has minimal security.

Obviously, these are two very different schools. They are worlds apart in terms of more than just geography. Throughout this book, we have highlighted the contextual differences within each school, their different equity priorities and foci, and the different social and political contexts within which they operate. We have also drawn attention to the different emphases framing our two research studies and their representation of Ridgeway and the Clementine-led alliance. We have examined the dynamics of leadership within one school, in the case of Ridgeway, and within one network, in the case of the Clementine-led alliance.

In this chapter we focus on the points of resonance within each of the case studies that are brought to light with the theoretical tools presented in this book. Our explicit engagement with the ethical dimensions of leadership and, especially, Foucault's ideas of truth-telling, counter-conduct and advocacy provide valuable insight into how school leaders might more effectively navigate the multifarious and uncertain terrain associated with the demands of the current climate. Despite the vastly different contextual and demographic circumstances in which school leaders might find themselves, we argue that these notions are critical when pursuing greater equity for all students.

The role of school leaders in contexts like Australia and England has never been more complex and difficult than it is at present. Whether leading one school or a network of schools, principals and head teachers are confronted with myriad new and ever-changing challenges and tensions, from the shifting needs of students arising from unprecedented levels of cultural diversity to the shifting expectations and heightened demands of the audit culture. While schools and their leaders are under greater surveillance than ever before, they are also more autonomous and self-managing. This context powerfully shapes educational leadership in relation to matters of equity and justice. As we have argued, it has rearticulated social justice and equity priorities in schools to a very narrow focus on what is measured: that is, students' achievements on a limited range of academic outcomes.

Throughout this book, we have stressed that school leadership must focus on more than this. If schools are to play a role in transforming the growing inequities of the social world, they must prioritise both the private and the public goals of education. They must support social efficiency and social mobility goals as well as democracy and citizenship. Such leadership work in the present climate demands an ethical approach that articulates an ideal or telos of leadership that is responsive to context and committed at its core to improving students' educational engagement and outcomes. Such a telos will support leaders to navigate ethically through the many, varied and complex moral codes or modes of subjection that both constrain and enable their work. Such ethical ways of leading demand an engagement with a political subjectivity of truth-telling, counter-conduct and advocacy. This is not to say that these kinds of ethical work are the only practices with which teachers should engage, but we believe that they need to form a core part of the ethos of leading schools in the current climate. They are important not only for disadvantaged schools like Ridgeway but for schools like Clementine, in terms of its responsibility to its own students and the students and communities of the other schools within the alliance.

A telos of leading for social justice

As we have stressed throughout this book, we are not concerned with articulating or prescribing what constitutes 'best' leadership practice. Rather, we have focused on how educational leaders might better understand and work with the complex and contradictory modes of subjection that shape their practice. It is this focus that makes transparent the ethical work of leaders in their critical analysis of these modes of subjection. Foucault's fourfold ethical framework is key here in providing the tools we need to understand and analyse these practices. Our concern in this book is with how such work might open possibilities for transformative and socially just leadership. Rather than prescribe solutions (something Foucault himself was loath to do), we have sought to illuminate the ethical work leaders conduct on themselves and on/with others towards their ideal or telos for leading their schools (in the case of Ridgeway) or networks (in the case of Clementine) in socially just ways.

In both of the case studies, issues of context are central to how a telos of leading for social justice is played out. Being sensitive and responsive to her school context is central to the principal at Ridgeway's telos of leadership. The type of principal Carol wishes to be involves adopting different leadership 'styles' to suit different situations. Sometimes this involves adopting a more authoritarian style when her school community seeks a firm decision; sometimes it involves a more distributive style in which she displays confidence in her team; and sometimes it involves a more 'servant' approach to leadership as a government officer reporting to her community. In Carol's view, she is not 'any one particular leader'. Rather, she adopts the most appropriate leadership style within the various modes of subjection shaping her work, whether from the community, her school or the government. Her leadership is situated within and responsive to multiple and competing discourses. There is no one way of working; and, in fact, there is a constant shifting and adaptation of her leadership approach based on the demands of the school context. Such demands shape Carol's subjectivity and the type of leader she wishes to be. She is, therefore, constantly in a process of becoming a principal or leader. We contend that this is a major feature of her leadership, and use the word 'becoming' because it suggests an ongoing process of subject formation of individuals rather than any assertion of what leaders are or should be. The formation of subjectivity is an endless process of construction, reconstruction and renegotiation of identities that are formed within particular historical, social, economic and cultural contexts, processes and discourses (Ball and Olmedo, 2013; Foucault, 2000). Carol's subject formation as the type of leader she wishes to be is contingent upon, and inscribed through, the school and community context. This context acts as a mode of subjection but also allows Carol some freedom to act according to her telos.

In defining her leadership in relation to social justice, Carol is in a process of becoming as she responds to the dynamics of context. The multiple and complex disadvantages confronting students at Ridgeway have prompted her to question her middle-class value system and back-ground. Such questioning leads to her developing what she describes as a 'more sophisticated' understanding of social justice that seeks to remove the barriers undermining her students' educational and social success. One of the key barriers she is trying to remove relates to poverty and the crime and unemployment that are associated with it. Carol's approach here is to ensure her school and students are adequately resourced to maximise learning, but also to challenge the deficit constructions and low expectations that have undermined her students' motivation and achievement at school. This approach, of course, generates tensions and requires Carol to conduct ethical work on both herself and others. In relation to student achievement, for example, Carol and the staff at Ridgeway must recognise, and work within, the demands of external modes of subjection, such NAPLAN. They must, at least to a degree, accept these as indicators of the school's 'success' in educating students. At the same time, Carol and her staff recognise that such modes of subjection: fail to capture the broad pastoral support the school offers students (especially the intense social and emotional support, given her students' highly disadvantaged backgrounds); and reinforce the deficit understandings associated with the school and its students that they are trying to challenge. For Carol and her staff, working ethically within these tensions is very difficult and often demoralising. While accepting these parameters, Carol navigates their tension by never losing sight of the school's emphasis on pastoral care and its significance in supporting the social, emotional *and* learning needs of her students.

Issues of context are also central in Clementine's leadership of the alliance. This leadership, like Carol's, is not fixed but fluid, shifting in response to the specifics of each school's context, which are shaped within various modes of subjection. For Clementine, an ethical way of leading the alliance within these parameters is to prioritise each school's autonomy and to foster collaboration between the schools. Important to this telos of leading is Clementine's rejection of an 'expert' or authoritarian style of relating to the other schools, because Ms J – Clementine's head teacher – understands that this would close down, rather than open up, opportunities within the alliance. Such a telos is seen as consistent with the parameters or modes of subjection of the National Teaching Schools initiative within which the alliance and its leadership are expected to operate as a mandate of the Department for Education. Ms J believes that these parameters are positive in their promotion of schools working together collaboratively in 'open' and 'genuine' ways. Through the provision of particular programmes, such as the Outstanding Teachers Programme (OTP), they enable a 'cascading of high-impact practice around and between schools' (Ms S) and create an environment in which all schools feel able to contribute to, and take from, the alliance. Crucially, there is no compunction for alliance schools to work with Clementine as a teaching school or to adopt programmes such as OTP. In this way, Clementine's leadership, and in particular the school's sensitivity to context and prioritisation of autonomy and collaboration, reflects the key elements that foster effective school networks – voluntary membership and flexible ties (Hargreaves, 2011).

Like Carol's telos of leadership, then, Clementine's leadership of the alliance is in a process of becoming. It is a way of working that is relational, ongoing and navigates through the particular social circumstances and/or modes of subjection that currently confront schools. Its focus on school autonomy and collaboration fosters the democratic conditions that are necessary if all schools in the alliance are to become active participants. Key here is Clementine's ethical approach to the modes of subjection shaping its leadership: that is, its approach to the authority it has been granted under the National Teaching Schools initiative. Rather than using this authority in oppressive or punitive ways (as it might have done), Clementine works to facilitate genuine collaboration with and between the other schools in the alliance in ways that respond to their individual needs and build on their individual capacities. Although we are concerned that the ethics of the parameters of the National Teaching Schools initiative have not been questioned in terms of their contribution to and strengthening of the broader market-oriented and undemocratic ideologies of the 'Big Society' upon which they are based, Clementine certainly does work ethically and justly within those parameters.

As with Carol's view of socially just leadership, the leadership of the alliance is directed towards supporting students to achieve, regardless of their background circumstances. Indeed, this is the group's stated 'moral imperative' and it is strongly endorsed by all alliance members. In contrast to Ridgeway, however, at Clementine there seems to be a more positive view and acceptance of external mandates of performance, such as exam results and Ofsted ratings, towards realising this goal. Powerful in shaping leadership behaviour and actions, these modes of subjection are seen by the Clementine-led alliance as constituting 'good' preparation 'for the next stage in [students'] lives' (Ms J) in terms of employment credentialing and ensuring students' future access to the labour market. Some members of the alliance (echoing Carol's opinion) have reservations about the narrowness of these measures. However, as one of the key purposes of the alliance (and evidence that it is doing its job) is to raise attainment on these measures, many schools expect membership of the group to help them achieve this. As such, they have embraced the formalised parameters mandated or sanctioned by the Department for Education that will support them in this pursuit, such as the peer-led, Ofsted-aligned evaluation of teaching and learning, the Quality Assurance Review. Of course, as at Ridgeway, working ethically within these modes of subjection generates tensions for Clementine, but in this case they are about maintaining its leadership telos of school autonomy and collaboration. These tensions, and their relevance to the processes of advocacy, truth-telling and counter-conduct, are the focus of the next section.

Advocacy, truth-telling and counter-conduct

At both Ridgeway and the Clementine-led alliance there are many ongoing tensions associated with navigating through the multifarious and difficult terrain of the current climate and, especially, the demands of the audit culture. Such tensions are related to Carol and Clementine maintaining their ethically driven telos of leadership and social justice within broader modes of subjection that threaten to undermine this ethical work. The leaders in both of these contexts are acutely aware of the high stakes of their work environments. For Carol, poor leadership performance (i.e. her school not reaching expected NAPLAN targets) could mean a termination of her contract. At Clementine, poor leadership (i.e. receiving an Ofsted grade of less than 'outstanding') would lead to the school losing its teaching school status. Such external and very public accountabilities not only reduce Ridgeway and Clementine and the work of its leaders to auditable commodities to be quantified, assessed and compared (and possibly found wanting), but discipline Carol and Ms J (at Clementine) to fit the profile of the ideal neoliberal subject. As we argued earlier, governmentality in its neoliberal form makes conducting others through the subject's own conduct one of its primary goals (Dardot and Laval, 2013; Foucault, 2007). Carol and the leaders at Clementine certainly govern their own conduct. Indeed, they are 'self-responsibilising' in this regard: that is, they position themselves within the broader modes of neoliberal subjection shaping their schools and their work as autonomous, self-determined and self-sustaining subjects who are solely responsible for successfully working within its parameters (see Shamir, 2008).

This positioning, of course, does not mean uncritically accepting these parameters with respect to what constitutes good schooling as both case studies clearly suggest. But it does place the responsibility for working ethically within these parameters squarely on the shoulders of school leaders. This is where the significance of ethical or moral leadership within the current environment becomes crucial in pursuing a social justice agenda in schools that is more than what is narrowly articulated around what is and what can be measured. In both school contexts, a strong commitment to advocacy and the practices of truth-telling and counter-conduct are instrumental in this pursuit.

For Carol, the high needs of her students drives her advocacy and her work in becoming a political subject. Circumstances of poverty, including poor housing and health as well as violence and criminality, are daily realities for her students. These realities shape Carol's political advocacy. She must provide the necessary level of care and support for her students so that they can access school and be available to learn. For Carol, this care and support is not separate from (indeed, it is crucial to) supporting her students to achieve on the measuring sticks that 'count' – educational performance benchmarks. The high needs of the students act as another important mode of subjection for Carol. While in tension with other modes of subjection, such as external public accountability, these are just as potent in shaping her leadership work.

Key to Carol's political subjectivity is challenging the deficit constructions and low expectations that have undermined her students' motivation and achievement at school. She is trying to change long-standing perceptions of the community and her students through 'social checking' of herself and her staff that deficit assumptions are challenged rather than reproduced, especially by ensuring high expectations of all learners and the provision of a 'rigorous' curriculum. She believes that the system has let her students down, so her role as advocate or political subject is directed towards changing the status quo, in which poverty invariably leads to educational failure. She challenges this system and the seeming lack of belief it has in students such as those at Ridgeway, but she also accepts responsibility for challenging the systems within her school. This challenging provides yet more evidence of her ethical self-conduct within broader modes of subjection.

A significant part of Carol's advocacy work for her students is evident in her truth-telling (parrhesia), which is a key aspect of her self-formation as principal. Her constitution of herself as a political subject is apparent in her efforts to improve the circumstances and opportunities of her Polynesian students. Speaking out about the ways in which modes of policy and governance silence or miss this group's particular social and educational needs (in relation to university access and healthcare) is a prime example of parrhesia. This involves a high level of risk for Carol, particularly given her short-term contractual status with Education Queensland, yet she feels it is important to speak the truth rather than allow a status quo that disadvantages her students to continue. Another way in which Carol engages in counter-conduct against the injustices of the status quo is through silence. This is evident when she refuses to mention or refer to policies and other forms of accountability that she believes do not help her students or the local community. For instance, Carol exercises power in her refusal to engage parents with the *MySchool* website. She dismisses its relevance, its capacity to capture the complex factors of disadvantage facing students at Ridgeway and its ability to evaluate the effectiveness or quality of the work done by herself and her staff at the school.

Leading as advocacy or political subjectivity within the Clementine-led alliance is associated with broader, systemic issues. The leaders of the member schools are concerned that the twin forces of autonomy and accountability within the education system are generating inequity by amplifying fragmentation, segregation, hierarchy and competition. In this high-stakes environment, 'good' schools (i.e. those that adhere to the narrow priorities of the high-stakes testing culture) are supposed to flourish, while 'bad' schools (i.e. those that are unable to succeed in this culture) are supposed to fail and disappear (see Apple, 2013). Members of the alliance are concerned that the prevalence of this ideology within their system is creating 'vulnerable' schools that are susceptible to the punitive measures associated with 'underperformance' (i.e. forced closure or 'take-over' by stronger schools). Such susceptibility is becoming even more of a concern with the continuing decline of local authority support (traditionally great assistance for state schools but increasingly a thing of the past within autonomised education systems).

Working ethically within this climate has entailed Clementine assuming an advocacy role to support the vulnerable schools in the alliance. These tend to be underperforming schools with challenging student demographics or small (primary) schools that have yet to become autonomised (i.e. convert to academy status) due to their lack of resources and management capacity. Within the parameters of the National Teaching Schools initiative, Clementine's advocacy or political subjectivity is directed towards seeking appropriate financial and moral support to ensure that these schools retain their autonomy and independence. Such support could be viewed as a form of counter-conduct as Clementine is acting against the injustices created through autonomised school environments to help vulnerable schools that face greater risks from the punitive measures of the audit culture than Clementine itself does.

It is Clementine's powerful position within and beyond the alliance – due to its status as an 'outstanding' teaching school – that allows it to engage in this counter-conduct in relation to external accountabilities. The leaders at Clementine, like Carol at Ridgeway, engage in parrhesia when speaking out against what they see as the grave inadequacies of Ofsted inspections in capturing the quality of teaching at the school. They are even willing to tell Ofsted that its inspections are not 'fit for purpose'. There is an element of risk in speaking up against the status quo in this way, given the deference to Ofsted's authority that is expected of English schools. However, the leaders at Clementine believe it is important to speak the truth rather than let a status quo that misrepresents their school continue unchallenged. Of course, there are strong parallels here with what motivates Carol to speak out at Ridgeway. Foucault's notion of counter-conduct being a key part of the formation of the self as an ethical subject is evident in these examples.

Further examples of counter-conduct are evident in the challenges to Clementine's leadership from *within* the alliance. Some member schools resist the standardisation and enterprise practices that Clementine promotes. For some of the leaders within the alliance, these practices prioritise economic imperatives over educative goals and detract from student learning. Some head teachers in the alliance argue that Clementine is more concerned with 'selling' products and offloading leadership responsibilities to protect its own financial position and status than with working towards the telos of leadership and social justice it espouses, especially in relation to ensuring school autonomy and fostering collaboration. This counter-conduct – in the form of speaking out against and seeking alternatives to Clementine's favoured practices – indicates significant tension within the alliance. The economic and standardisation imperatives to which Clementine subscribes (and which some of the member schools resist) are all directives or modes of subjection within the National Teaching Schools initiative. All of the schools within the alliance are expected to operate within these modes of subjection, even though they are likely to compromise the group's ethical leadership approach. Hence, we feel that the questioning of these parameters by some member schools is heartening in social justice terms. These schools are displaying a recognition of how the parameters can play out in ethically unsound and unjust ways in terms of their market orientation; their propensity to encourage undemocratic relations; and their promotion of standardised, prescriptive and decontextualised frames for what might constitute teacher quality and improvement. Indeed, several of them have adopted alternatives that have opened spaces for understanding teaching as a more complex, situated and intellectual activity, rather than a set of 'practical' and 'relevant' skills that can be prescribed, qualified and evaluated.

Conclusion

While worlds apart in many respects, there are clear points of resonance within the leadership practices at Ridgeway State High School and the Clementine-led alliance. These points of resonance, as illuminated throughout this book with reference to the work of Foucault, offer significant insight into how schools might more justly navigate through the multiple and difficult challenges of today's education environment. Despite their vastly different contextual and demographic circumstances, leaders in Ridgeway and the alliance are working towards a telos of socially just leadership that is contextually responsive and a telos of socially just schooling that is committed to improving the educational outcomes of all students. It is clear that pursuing these teloi is far from easy. Carol is working within and against the dire conditions of poverty, violence and crime that undermine her students' school participation and engagement. She is trying to support her school and community to think beyond the deficit understandings of her students that strengthen the link between poverty and school/life failure. And she is doing all of this amid broader modes of subjection that seem to thwart her every move, such as external accountability measures that fail to capture crucial elements of her school's social/pastoral care work and equity policy that fails to include, and thus support, the special needs of her students.

At Clementine, the complexities and difficulties associated with pursing a telos of socially just leadership are associated with efforts to foster school autonomy and collaboration within similar external accountability demands and other modes of subjection. Shaped and governed by the parameters of government policies such as the National Teaching Schools initiative and programmes such as OTP, Clementine is responsible for leading and supporting the improvement of every school in the alliance while also maintaining its own status and capacity as an 'outstanding' teaching school.

The stakes at both Ridgeway and Clementine in terms of their leaders effectively navigating through such modes of subjection are extremely high – 'poor' leadership performance in either context will surely result in great personal and professional loss. Amid, and perhaps in resistance to, these demands, the leadership at Ridgeway and Clementine prioritises ethical ways of working. Leading in these environments is a relational process and thus never fixed or prescriptive as it is always mindful of, and responsive to, context. It is, nevertheless, specific in its social justice agenda or telos. It is firmly directed towards creating the conditions of care and democracy necessary for pursuing better outcomes for all students within the present climate, where it is extremely difficult to create such conditions. This pursuit, of course, does not entail a rejection of the broader high-stakes environment and the narrow external measures that constitute school effectiveness. In both contexts, for example, the equity significance of students' achievement on these measures is openly acknowledged. The point is that such broader modes of subjection – whether in the form of leadership policy, teacher improvement programmes or standardised accountability regimes – are engaged with *critically* both at Ridgeway and within the Clementine-led alliance. This critical engagement, crucially, has led to a strong commitment in both contexts to advocacy and the practices of parrhesia and counter-conduct. This commitment and these practices are seen as instrumental in leading justly and ethically within and against the modes of subjection that shape these schools.

As we have illustrated throughout this book, such Foucauldian concepts not only help us to understand the complex ways in which leaders work on themselves and others but open up opportunities to conceptualise leadership in different ways from those that are most prevalent within the leadership field. We have employed Foucault's theories on ethics and the formation of the subject because these have been less fully explored than other aspects of his work. They also allow us to demonstrate *productive* forms of power, while so many others continue to focus on discipline and control – the negative aspects of power in education.

In our two case studies, this productive use of power is particularly evident in the ways in which advocacy, truth-telling and counter-conduct are mobilised against the inequities of the broader status quo. For Carol at Ridgeway, this is about ensuring that her students are provided with the social and material support they need to access and participate at school; it is about high expectations and a rigorous curriculum; and it is about speaking out against dismissive and unfair policies and accountability that further marginalise her students and her school. For the Clementine-led alliance, the productive use of power to challenge the status quo is about providing the requisite social and material support for 'vulnerable' schools so that they may continue to exist and retain a degree of autonomy; it is about speaking out against the inadequacies of Ofsted's inspections; and it is about member schools speaking out against aspects of Clementine's leadership that they feel compromise their own schools' autonomy and success.

The concepts of advocacy, truth-telling and counter-conduct are particularly useful in generating new lines of thinking in relation to leadership and the *critical* work involved in self-conduct. We have focused on the ongoing processes involved in leaders working on themselves and others in pursuit of their telos of social justice through such advocacy work and the productive use of power in this process. Importantly, this has involved the leaders at Ridgeway and Clementine critically reflecting on their own (privileged) ways of viewing marginalised students and schools. At Ridgeway, Carol reflects on how her relatively advantaged upbringing and background compare with the poverty and crime that are prevalent in her students' lives and the local community. She recognises that her background frames her leadership and her views of the students, so she consciously disrupts – and supports her teachers to disrupt – these privileged views in the hope of halting further reproduction of deficit understandings of the Ridgeway school community. At Clementine, such critical reflection is evident at a broader level, with Ms J's understanding that its privileged status as an 'outstanding' teaching school could alienate member schools if it is employed in punitive and oppressive ways. Disrupting this privilege is apparent in Clementine's efforts to foster genuine collaboration with and between the other schools in the alliance.

It is clear that these leaders are working in socially just ways with an explicit focus on supporting students and communities to overcome disadvantage. How they go about doing this should give us all food for thought about the contemporary experience for school leaders and the ways in which they must grapple with the current constraints of their work, as well as the spaces where they can exercise resistance and counter-conduct. Of course, we respect these leaders and the work they are doing, but we do not valorise them as the answer to education's problems. We understand that this may not be a popular approach, but it is one that allows for a more nuanced understanding of the complex processes involved in leading for social justice. The case studies may be from England and Australia, but we hope that the theoretical tools will generate ways of thinking about and practising leadership for social justice across much broader contexts, so that educational leadership not only as a field but as a form of practice will continue to engage critically with the challenges of working in diverse and disadvantaged contexts towards greater social equity and justice for all.

References

Apple, M. (2013). *Can education change society?* New York, Routledge.

Ball, S. J. and Olmedo, A. (2013). Care of the self, resistance and subjectivity under neoliberal governmentalities. *Critical Studies in Education*, 54 (1), 85–96.

Dardot, P. and Laval, C. (2013). *The new way of the world: On neoliberal society*. London, Verso.

Foucault, M. (2000). The ethics of the concern for self as a practice of freedom. In P. Rabinow (ed.) *Essential works of Foucault 1954–1984*, Volume I: *Ethics*. London, Penguin.

Foucault, M. (2007). *Security, territory, population: Lectures at the College de France 1977–1978*. New York, Picador.

Hargreaves, D. (2011). System redesign for system capacity building. *Journal of Educational Administration*, 49 (6), 685–700.

Shamir, R. (2008). The age of responsibilization: On market embedded morality. *Economy and Society*, 37 (1), 1–19.

Index